poems for teeth

Richard Loranger

Artwork by Eric Waldemar
and the author

We Press
2005

We Press
P.O. Box 436
Allamuchy, NJ 07820

www.wepress.org

AUTHOR'S EMAIL: mythkiller@hotmail.com

Excerpts from "Edentulous Fantasy" and "Tooth of Myth"
appeared in "Eats and Drinks", a dining column by Jennifer
Blowdryer for the *New York Press*, October 5, 2004.

Cover x-rays by Deborah Pasquale.
Cover design, teeth chart, and book design by the author.

This edition includes calligraphic art by
Eric Waldemar
on the title page and pages 8, 20, 32, 44, 56, 68, 74, 80, 104,
116, 134, 158, 164, and 176,
and by
Richard Loranger
on pages 2, 14, 26, 38, 50, 62, 86, 92, 98, 110, 122, 128, 140,
146, 152, 170, and 182.

Check out more art at www.ericwaldemar.com.

To

Deborah Pasquale, D.D.S.,

for
patience,
skill,
and kindness
beyond the call

teeth

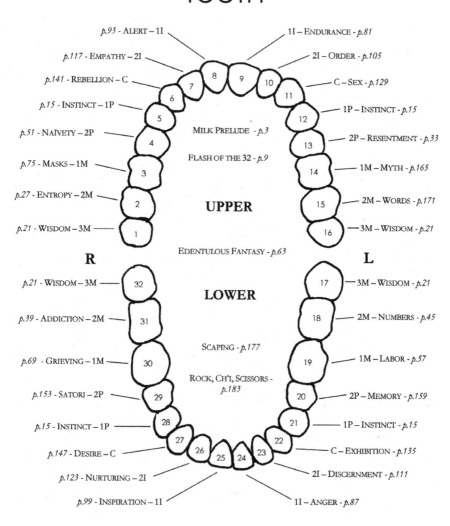

p.93 - ALERT – 1I

p.117 - EMPATHY – 2I

p.141 - REBELLION – C

p.15 - INSTINCT – 1P

p.51 - NAÏVETY – 2P

p.75 - MASKS – 1M

p.27 - ENTROPY – 2M

p.21 - WISDOM – 3M

1I – ENDURANCE - p.81

2I – ORDER - p.105

C – SEX - p.129

1P – INSTINCT - p.15

2P – RESENTMENT - p.33

1M – MYTH - p.165

2M – WORDS - p.171

3M – WISDOM - p.21

MILK PRELUDE - p.3

FLASH OF THE 32 - p.9

UPPER

EDENTULOUS FANTASY - p.63

R

L

LOWER

SCAPING - p.177

ROCK, CH'I, SCISSORS - p.183

p.21 - WISDOM – 3M

p.39 - ADDICTION – 2M

p.69 - GRIEVING – 1M

p.153 - SATORI – 2P

p.15 - INSTINCT – 1P

p.147 - DESIRE – C

p.123 - NURTURING – 2I

p.99 - INSPIRATION – 1I

3M – WISDOM - p.21

2M – NUMBERS - p.45

1M – LABOR - p.57

2P – MEMORY - p.159

1P – INSTINCT - p.15

C – EXHIBITION - p.135

2I – DISCERNMENT - p.111

1I – ANGER - p.87

contents

LOST TEETH

Pending Teeth

AUTHOR'S NOTE

I have my mother's eyes and teeth. Her eyes are beautiful. Her teeth are mostly artificial. A few of mine are of that brilliant blend of sand, metal, and fire, some partly so, but quite a few are just plain gone. These poems are their story, at least in part, but they're also about your teeth, and everyone's for that matter, as well as a few other things.

Teeth fall out. It's part of the human – er, mammalian – er, vertebrate condition. It's been happening for geologic ages. We deal with it. Still, you'd think that in *this* day and age, there'd be a stop to it, a tooth preserver, some dental panacea. The thing is, it's not so much for a lack of dental technology that we still have dental problems – the technology is there, but the behavior is not. I could have much healthier teeth if I had taken better care of them, *and* if I lived in a society that didn't reserve decent medical care as a privilege of class, that didn't value money over human lives. Wishful thinking, in *this* day and age, and all the more as the minutes tick by. The state of our teeth reflects the state of our cultures, our selves, our politics, our psyches, our bodies, and just about every other thing subject to human follies and flaws, foibles and corruption, at least that I can think of, anyway.

I have generally held jobs which, at least by economic standards, are considered relatively useless in our culture – waiting tables, bike messaging, painting, temping, and now teaching college-level English as an adjunct lecturer, and thus have almost never had insurance of any kind. So like those of over 40 million other Americans, my teeth have been shown the proverbial door. By my late thirties, I'd become known as such a wealth of dental…wisdom, that more and more people asked why I didn't write about my teeth. I generally shrugged, and suggested that

I didn't have anything particularly new to say about them. My experience, though trialsome, is far from unique, and I felt that any tome or ditty about my little troubles would read only as a fancy whine that many an unprivileged citizen could justly voice. It would take a bit more than another toothache to change my mind about that.

More than another toothache came in 2002 in the form of a jaw infection that took a year of my health and one of the few molars that I had left. I could barely chew, and I was looking at thousands of dollars worth of work if I ever wished to masticate joyfully again. All this on the budget of an adjunct in debt. So I decided to make a chapbook of funny little poems about teeth, to sell for a $10 donation towards fixing them. This plan may have worked well, except that once I finally started writing about teeth, mine or otherwise, the floodgates gaped, and instead of a month's worth of funny little poems, for over two years out came the crazy odes that you'll find here.

Though this book follows the crucible of my own mouth, doling grief for teeth lost and hope for those remaining, feel free to ignore that and read it however you like. You will note that to each of the teeth I have assigned a quality, a riff of sorts off the wisdom teeth – Tooth of Anger, Tooth of Myth, Teeth of Instinct, and the like. These assignations are not from some arcane or esoteric source, nor are they a long-lost trump of metaphysic or divination; I gathered them from what I see every day, and that is all. The teeth are not a system. They are teeth. These poems are not a system. They are thank-yous. Thank-yous to my teeth. And thank *you* as well for checking them out. Have a nice teeth.

Richard Loranger
June 9, 2005

Teeth hadst thou in thy head when thou wast born, to signify thou cam'st to bite the world.
- William Shakespeare

What is't that ails young Harry Gill?
That evermore his teeth they chatter,
Chatter, chatter, chatter still!
- William Wordsworth

A Tooth upon Our Peace
The Peace cannot deface—
Then Wherefore be the Tooth?
- Emily Dickinson

Americans may have no identity, but they do have wonderful teeth.
- Jean Baudrillard

poems for teeth

When our very lives are threatened,
we begin to live.

Henry Miller

Milk Prelude

Erupting from the mandible,
the daughters of the blade
begin to sing:

Slice, willy-nilly,
slam, crush n grind
until you find your way into
the sheer wild world.

The cartilage becomes your dream,
the dream, a living fact of rock and canker,
fantasy and chance, torque that canticles
and finds
flowers brewing in the unkempt mind.

Deep in this cave
a tiny creature breaks through the wall,
a breeze breaks in,
and the stone hand of an ancient bas-relief
resting here for ages
starts to move.

Your eyes slide open
beneath a veil of clay.
An unseen ally tears the film,
and teases vision into day.

What nascent rock abides, child,
what ooze calcifies and blooms
nearly weightless and transplendent
with last dregs of the mist?

What fierce cooing do you hear
deep in the roots of antiphon?

Maxilla answers with a cry
breaching bounds of latch and nerve:

Smash, shimi shimi,
crash, crack n smile,
and find your fill and fall into
the dark, dark hole.

The primal children gather
in a game of spear and clash —
piercing fracas, shrill dismay, false alarms
resounding still with glee and sotted through
with sugar logs and lemonade,
motley all around and laughing to the roofs
of old garages — calls and clamor,
fireflies, darting minds,
a sandbox fray, battle cries,
rattle for position, wild eyes,
wry wit sung, balls fly, confetti flung,
and bit lips wrung — taste this
salt of effort and anthem on the hill
as the troops melee, charge and dodge,
tackling, tussling, waving arms,
stamping, cheering, leaping for that slim
diurnal moon and variously
cantering on the precipice
where rocks shift, grass grows thin,
and all the sky is a carnival.

Deep within the torque begins.

Who can ignore precocious play
lifting from the limbs and joints,
ligaments aching for the stretch,
teething gums, raking nails,
thickening soles that love the pound,
the taste of sun, the surging veins
sprouting in dense game
on a deep deciduous plain —
O milk, O gleam
of endless summer days,
of sated alleycats
betrayed by a few shorn seasons,
molted, torn, unceremoniously
spat by brick itself —
on a rock the size of an orchard
slipping, slipping from the coast
into the alga and ague
of honking cars, intermittent rain,
the smiles of an unreadable dream
hung on the rack of a well-worn tome.

Welcome to the island: it is your bone.

Flash of the 32

Bite me.

You
    stinking

Eye tooth rises
    I see you
and behind, a brood of
    vaguely

Awake, fresh ones, to pounce,
song of union
anxious but rising
to city, island, pack, myth, tone.
Awake and rear, ardent compendium
torquing with hormone, hungry
for first
kill —

    Smile big now

Half a gleam and half a pall
rise within the burning eye
Saliva wets the tensing jaw
Hold back, hold back

For an hour
all present,
all possible,
the creatures find themselves
in sensate wilderness
urgent, honed, nearly sybillic,
brazen —
nothing shakes the granite heart
pulsing the
sweet acrid cells of hunt:

Away, away with childish things
and off to fields of victory,
away to ribbons, rants, and reels,
a pot of meat and mead for all!

Smell that hot
            prey

You are a wolf's grin and you are
maniacal, flooded
with such sharp
curl'd lip of
meat love,
blades sprung,
mouth of steel,
the scent
filling blood with
sight:
the banker in the corner,
the harridan at the stove,
two hare in a culvert
and a grouse not to take flight —

      Gotta have it
huh huh

Champing hot breath,
the 32 debate the spring:
one for the rank taste,
one for the quick slice,
one for the high cry,
one for the slow grind...

Two worlds eager
to collide,
the jaw a clutch of
clash
that sees the end of jaw

and laughs, drunken

— with flight, with speed,
with adrenal joy
and for an hour
readiness

flashing

a grin
fabulous with
heat and the seductive
charm of the beast
disarming and illusive
twisting and marking
you bared for the
fang

flashing

one throng gleaming
in the dusk shimmering
into many one many
pinnacles
canticles
vitalities
waiting
like a Tarot deck or I Ching sticks
to be spilled across the table

flashing

a brief
tortuous glimpse of
the mass mental
the perfect teem
before beset upon
before we isolate
the tender, sweet, careening
citizens of the womb.

TEETH OF INSTINCT

5, 12, 28, 21 – FIRST PREMOLARS

Perhaps it is fitting that #5 should be the first to go,
since 5 would later whisper so insistently. Not that we
can't find allies in all numbers, but there is something
special, something uncanny in 5. 5's. And E's.
Something that flashes. Something that unravels.

And they do not die, none of them, I should say that
right off — they go, and stay; and in going, rear, and
in staying, splay. But they all, eventually, go.

Without warning,
in a community of lawns and trees,
ice cream trucks, summer skies —
bridges blown,
toys shattered,
girders snapped,
cables severed.

The arm of the machine descends.
What crass cause seeks the rivet?
What pattern does it seek to quell?

5 runs blithely through a field
smelling old trees, wild reeds,
fresh dung, dirt, road, town —
gives a whistle; others gather in the tall grass.
They are the Know-It-All Club,
the Secret Shift of Do As We Will,
and as a member each attempts to live,
to light the day come sun or no,
to dance like mad through the midnight streets,
and as a member each obliquely *does*,
opens arms to make the world,
dives the rapids underground,
and will en-joy you better believe.
12 is the wheel-master; eats dirt and lives;
embraces his shadow like there's no tomorrow;
knows every wrench in the book in the dark;
leaps out of trees; breaks into basements.
21 is the task-master; is good with knives;
loves colors; makes lists;
recalls data with stunning finesse;
eats paper; has fifteen cyberselves.

28 is the musician; eats fire;
can't tell instrument from mind;
changes names to meet his mood;
knows time and space; has a hell of a card collection.
And 5 is the ring-master, catenator,
master-schemer, maker of maps;
takes long hikes late at night;
knows the art of every knot;
eats greens; loves to dance;
solves puzzles; is happy with everyone.

They are the weird kids,
outcasts, upstarts, sniffers, spies,
live wires, truth speakers, bone seekers,
they slide beneath, perch, pass notes, decode,
they watch, know the town by smell,
know every corner, crack, and crease,
they read all sides of the leaf —
they are nutrient, enzyme, centerspring,
dendrite, conduit, invisible bridge,
keystone, palate, continent,
they introduce the town to tectonics,
to itself,
and the town recoils.

Guess what happens next.

The cloak drops; camera snicks;
hail cracks the windowpanes;
nerves staunched by coca and the blade.

Order and beauty will commence.
Pardon the inelastic reins.

There are no symbols here,
just shards of calcium and lives
(a pattern, reflected, multiplied,
magnified, charging through grass,
through the windblown streets),
a hankering for symmetry,
a paring of a spur,
the wreaking of a citizen,
and reaping of incontinent minds.

Fear! Fire! Foes!
Machines! Marauders! Jackdaws!
Untimely ripp'd!
Untimely ripp'd!

Teeth of Wisdom

17, 32, 16, 1 – Third Molars

How doth the hunter hew and hack,
leaving some to starve?

Four young girls are chosen
for deep roots and sharp eyes,
for sensate brows
and strong spines,
chosen each generation
by the order
to bear the lore of the town,
to preserve the ancient catechism,
the writ that spells rule.
The order seeks
the old ensconced in the new
as a vehicle for itself,
and this time it has made very good choices.

17 is teasing her hair and thinking of physics.
Each hair flares with a charge
that lights another thought and feels the air.
A car pulls up outside her window....
32 is smoking behind a convenience store,
laughing with friends playing truth or dare.
Each choice excites equally – she takes a dare.
She hasn't time to spritz her breath for the two men
    approaching....
16 is swimming with all her indefatigable heart.
Her body responds to the water with grace and union.
With each lap she is more ready for the current.
They wait at the end of the pool like a waterfall....
And 1, most plain, most serious, opens the mind
in the guise of a senior psychology spree.
She will determine how thoughts are conceived.
She knows they are coming before they arrive....
It is spring. They are all preparing
for a graduation unlike that
for which they prepare.

What begets the perverse adulation
of a familiar pale?

Here is the dark giggle of the tale:
they're so well chosen,
each channeling hungry visions, that once convened
old sight meets new light and they begin to chew,
they feed each other, fall in love,
they spend all night inventing their own world,
all day promoting their design,
their own birthright looms as a new horizon
rolling toward the old town a moon-sized mote.

These are the pearls,
irritants in the soft tissue
coated with nacre in self-defense,
calcified, objectified, renamed
for the beauty of the coating,
for layered salve.
Are these grains of sand
intrusion of the world,
peaks impaling dogs,
or mixed life,
part of a greater organ?

Integrity of the order is threatened.
An emergency meeting is called.
Propriety cannot permit termination,
but they must be somehow removed, expulsed,
exiled for preservation
of the long-borne gong.

What can explain the brute predilection
to catapult the strange?

The preservative party lays down the law:
17's plunked in a think-tank,
32's tossed in a cave,
1 is encased in a gallery,
16 is stuffed in a window display:
all fined, all revered,
all cantilevered clear.

Deep in a cave there is a secret,
a shiny stone.
You put it there ages ago
and forgot about it.

Where can we look for a simple recant
for the violence man causes man?

White is for purity and death in Japan
Bring me a scalpel as fast as you can
Where is the hidden, delectable white,
the oldest and youngest teeth of the night

Tooth of Entropy

#2 – Upper Right 2ND Molar

I dunno what the danger is, but I
will figure it out eventually, I'm sure,
as soon as I relax a bit, and then
I'll take a look at everything again.
It's just a matter of letting matters slide
along, if you can stand to sit that long,
and then sometimes I think I've gotta find
somethin better to occupy my time.

Ne'er a molar ever was
like indolent Mr. 2,
brave as a fish,
twice as rich,
and thrice as oopsy-doo.

Oopsy-doo
  Oopsy-doodle
    Oopsy cock-a-doodle-doo
When the clock hit the poodle
    I didn't know what to do

2 thinks about furniture.
He's been sitting here a long time, and has seen
the room chew chairs like a mad gerbil.

I like my coffee table a lot.
It's where I put my magazines and shit.
Lint fascinates me – I can't tell whether it's a sign
of things coming together
or things falling apart.
Philosophy exhausts me.
Sometimes I stare at peeling paint for hours.
Some people think it's cause I'm stoned, but really
I'm just letting all the factors drift into place.
That's the ticket.

Oopsy-dee
  Oopsy-deedle
    Oopsy diddle-deedle-dum
If you sleep with a beetle
    you might just be a bum

2 thinks about weather —
one of his favorite topics, really.
It happens every day, he's noticed,
like free cable.

My favorite channel is The Weather Channel.
I could watch it 24-7.
There's nothin like a good storm watch,
and the earthquake specials are the best.
I never knew earthquakes were weather before.
It just goes ta show ya.
One time tornadoes came right through town.
They showed pictures of green sky and horizontal rain
right down the street from my house.
They told me to hide in my closet,
but that was must-see TV.

Oopsy-ding
   Oopsy-dingle
      Oopsy ding-a-ling-a-ling
When the wind hit the mountain
      all the rocks began to sing

2 thinks a lot about hills.
He's been reading about a hot debate
as to whether hills should be classified
according to the manner of the scarp,
the way rock loosens from the slope,
or the manner of the pediment,
the croppings formed of sediment.

This is one thing I can talk authoritatively on.
I subscribe to *National Geo* and everything.
It's kind of like the lint thing.
Of course things crumble, and of course
the rubble ends up at the bottom.
I just don't see why they gotta argue about it.
Why is one more important than the other?
What's the big frickin deal?
It's all just gravity.
One thing I'll say about hills, though,
they're nice to look at, anyway.

Said the scarp to the pediment,
    "Slide! Slide!"
to which the pediment replied,
    "Why? Why?"

2 looks in the mirror and says,
"Who are you?"
And all his teeth drop out.
Except the canines.

Oopsy-doopsy   floopsy-whoopsy
woozy-twosy   inna chute
Bouncy-flouncy   slidesy-widesy
lucksy-ducksy   whadda dupe

Hopsy-slopsy   numbsy-thumbsy
headsy-firsty   inna dive
Splatsy-flatsy   cracksy-wacksy
byesy-whysy   spap oop.

TOOTH OF RESENTMENT

#13 – UPPER LEFT 2ND PREMOLAR

What grin bears a dark within?
All grins, but the grin of 13
reflects a darkness too.
13 stands by the podium in his study,
tapping, tapping at the wood
with well-pared nails —
admits no shadow,
cannot bear the stains
afflicted by the world,
and thus becomes its mirror.

And what a mirror does, the earth does,
scored as the face of man
by acids and the hail
of malice, bitter partings,
and occluded fronts.
But while earth crumbles, as we know,
recycling to igneous,
13 resists,
surrounds himself with thick bone, stone staves,

accretes an ivory cave
and grips, grips like hell.
Ahh, sweet humans.

Grip, grip, and grit
Grip, grip, and grit
Ahh shit
Another chip

That burns me up.

For in teeth, as in earth, as in us,
inside the darkness there is burning, burning,
scourge and cleanse, digestion, reinvention, unless
soul clench its holes and freeze, and further seize
and seal all ports, his life
a geode filled with ash and quartz,
insulated, safe, detached from harm,
in a word, petrified.

13 ricochets about the chamber
scoring theorems of his own reprise,
a prisoner to pulse and mind,
his rants resounding in the citadel
an œuvre to introspect.

For a time, he becomes the town enigma,
taunted by daring kids, bantered by adults,
shunned by all but a fearless few.

Who goes there?
A friendly tooth.
Whaddaya want?
To hear your song.
Go away.

Clench, clench, and cinch
Clench, clench, and cinch
Ahh me
How to free

The seized monkey.

Fire without influx
either smothers
or cracks the shell and consumes.
Long ago 13 oxidized within,
singed without forging,
and now the inferno, which must reinvent, vents
through the nearest gape and sets the face aflame,
eyes sear, brow blackens,

the monkey morphs into a dragon,
the throat a furnace of remorse,
the grin a forest of flaming teeth,
each word a blaze
scorching the unfortunate.

Rear, rear, and sear
Rear, rear, and sear
Ahh dear
Why to fear

The freshening air.

Ignited, 13 becomes a nuisance,
a pyretic poison at the hamlet's core
that must be purged.

Knock, knock.
Who's there?
Nobody but a rotting house
lodged in the bedrock.

The extraction takes hours.
13 won't let go,
hangs hot to the bone

gripping and moaning,
spewing shards and mud,
fuming reflection,
shattering sense,
snapping wit and pith,
sardonic to the quick
and snarl dark.

TOOTH OF ADDICTION

31 – LOWER RIGHT 2ND MOLAR

Addiction tooth loves the chew,
the sexy ache, tender pressure of the socket
juicing next the thought, next move, next panache,
panoply, giddy gnash, gimme gimme what could possibly
galaxy spinning like a splendid spun-glass spectrum
unfolding mind face these thoughtful hands
eyes like wrecking balls slurping the next
gorgeous languid gorge of straight up
pulp and all O sweet is there a cup
for all this vessel vein dray
canal cauldron reservoir sluice
bitter chalice of
but what chalice is
Are you the chalice?
Is it?
Brux, brux, brux away
a hundred thoughts, a thousand bones —
lux, lux, lux of ciliation
is your only home

39

Lux my ass
cupping the surge light
tilling bitter into child come come
gnashing one, the light of root peals —
here you are the man this is your ground too
soon the pretty carnal engine chewing on
wet shiny animal heart chewing the stark
animal mind loving the snarl hunting
some staring chunk of the sooty
goddamned planet chewing
on its own regret begets a sharp
little friend telling of the turnkeys
turning dust into a catapult
give mere protoplasm
seek the glaring charm
receive the O O my
can you need
more?
Brux, brux, brux away
the candied lack, the shiny shoe —
crux, crux, crux of satiation
is the root of you

Gnash and breathe, the urge
meats the horny coddle of the lanky whore
thrumming two fleshy pads on a crest of wanton
marrow in the veins, hot bone, pectin, rush of axe,
bereavedom — cut the shit, how's a little globba
caffeine scotch codeine power applause nicotine
heroin ritalin sex lager valium respect conflict
money methydrine sugar sugar sugar up the
medulla oblongata
throbbing a thick yes into
do it you
piece of
Brux, brux, brux away
the urgent nerve – the molten clay
fucks, fucks, fucks a castigation
of the fading day
draining
the drear light of
lovely cantilever
cracking the wild
sweet, sweet tooth
into *delirare*

furrowed and sublime
ledge unravelling
a glimpse of pure
recalcitrant
love —
Hang on, tooth,
this is quite a
sharp
bits and pieces
darting
I brought a
horse to do my
bidding and
dragged back
a shed skin
tail on the
floor
creaking under the
dear
everything
drained and drifting
whole knot

strained and
one strand
snaps
and
shows the spreading sky ———
Bye-bye, addiction tooth.
Bye-bye.

Tooth of Numbers

#18 – Lower Left 2ND Molar

Deceptive, deceptive,
must have a candy,
thinks in a shoebox,
boxes, boxes

ratcheting, ratcheting,
can't find the ceiling,
must have an orderly
rainbow, rainbow

Once upon a time there was a
big man in a little house who
collected all the ants. He had a vision
to create the biggest peacock ever
out of ants. Sooner or later the ants
didn't live up to his expectations and were
let go. This man lived in a
house of numbers.

So decisive the ant,
unwavering though occluded.
So incisive children,
before the tinted film.
So precise the diamond,
a wonder of ferns left to the wind.
So honed the ear,
to find the hidden hen.
Even the genteel caesura,
a measured machination of me.

Precision the mystery,
                    the attraction,
                              the deception.

earwig, earwig
lives in a diagram,
thinks it's a palace,
can't sing, can't sing

After a hollow time he is taken in
by a siren who promises
all the shoes in the world if only
he can count them. He takes
sweet sweet solace sanctum solace
counting counting chanting counting
the mounting mound of shoes hewn
from the skins of flowers and babes by
you, desire, you insouciant bitch
with whom we are not yet through,
though you may be through with
lean 18, feverish, sleepless, frantic-
ally tracking, all precision
in the balance, scratching
the first doomed tentacles of script
on a fading boxtop,
cross the marble flank of a storehouse,
on his own bones, brittle,
unsated, burning, running
heated hands over scrimshaw
accounts of murder by the book.

echoey, echoey,
poor hungry eyeball
hides in a brainscope,
torrid, torrid

18 retreats to a lightless room
where he contemplates a table filled with artifacts.
They are his language, his future, his retention:
bits of china, shiny things from the street, an old plastic
wrench, a peanut shell, a glass bell, a blade....
He is thinking of just one thing:
Given the right conditions, a leaf could slice through granite.
He rolls an old eraser absentmindedly
across the tabletop. He grabs a glass of milk.
A leaf hangs from a beech in Mississippi,
pumping sun to cells, sugar to the trunk.
He sits with an unseen lump of coal in his hand,
gripping, ungripping—sniffs it.
Splays both palms flat on the cool surface.
The leaf lets go, hovers a moment pirouetting
like any other leaf, takes a dive, and drifts into rock.
He belches silently and long, has a little heartburn today.

18 is not the sudden song,
not the alchemist fiddling with charms,
not the furious lover who makes a paper flower;
it is the relentless storm, the mountaineer
who must scale every peak.
It is the tooth chewing through quartz.

18 drifts off
in a gust of numbers,
limbs splayed and
singing to the stars,
a mechanical leaf
in a rockless breeze.

canticle, canticle,
numbers and feathers
can't be distinguished,
lovely, lovely

Tooth of Naïvety

#4 – Upper Right 2ND Premolar

Wide-eyed and trammeled,
even at this age, wide-eyed,
luscious and freshbrained,
fresh pickins, so prime cut
even a falling star becomes
a sailing farthing, searing
mums, fire's eye, truth,
a hurtling tooth.

Wide-eyed knows the island and the shale,
looks at city hall
and sees a big honkin pile of repartee,
looks at flowers and sees
flowers, not the monsters they're cracked up to be,
can't be rained on,
plays the pretty little butterfly-man
child child not child
teeming with whirring-wings and tall-towers
not for watching but

for looking and whirring and delirious wide-eyed darts
darts into the dry hay
dusk husking the day into such clear air
and look over there
the first bright car lights the evening sky and
wide-eyed sees a simple song
ringing a path of peace through the patriside.

Too bad wide-eyed gotta slide,
with all that uumph who wouldn't wanna
wheel in the chicken,
snatch a quick check,
buy the big farm and farm the big guy,
tell a tale for a tail,
grin big and grab arm
twist nose pull hair bare claw
smash tooth rip eye get it get it
submit you little
pupil
and wide-eyed is gouged, robbed, left to pickle
in his own remittance,
preserved for posterity and a few mean tasks,
relieved to put the truth on ice,
rectified that writhing = freedom,
that squinting sharps the view,

that heartrot is a necessary phew.
And through all this,
stunned but unexcoriated,
wide-eyed lives, and strives,
and keeps a caring eye,
thinks wide and dreams,
means what he sees
and says what he means.

And wide-eyed means
lots of sparks in the wind and
pictures of ladies in the grass and
thousands of new ways to clean a lug
and they all work.
And rivers and moonbeams
and tugboats and flies and skies
full of hope and people building bridges
and eating corn and sharing their drawings
and touching each other and even worse
wide-eyed says something about it
and this is unacceptable
believing is one thing but reeving is another
and wide-eyed is yanked, hurtled, sent
smacking, heaved heapward.

And even hurtling, even still,
wide-eyed rears a simple joyous trill
of peace through the ever-lovin runting-side.

Give me a moment,
a moment with a blade of grass
under the sun
and I'll remember who I am.

Show me a rock
so I can find a continent
just big enough
to dance with all my friends.

Give me a shoe
that I may visit everything
and have a home
wherever I may find myself.

Show me a world
where no one ever tells a lie.
I have a right
to live with all my might.

And wide-eyed is right.

Tooth of Labor

19 – Lower Left 1ST Molar

A toll.
A toll.
Insurrection and enough.

Crumbling sand.
Crumbling shells.
A breach of.

There is a violence in the order of things
that shows itself in multiplicities,
a violence in every breath
that can be overcome
only by breathing
and knowing it.

Some heroes are acclaimed for sweeping
the flesh from the fire.
19's heroism runs deeper, accretes from below,
a stalagmitic fortitude of ground, his devotion
to building the house.

19 labors.

19 works like a dog-gone dog
for fealty to form and family —
he toils against the moil, against the flail
of entropy, starts and torques, fumbles and rails —
ain't no saint by far, has his crappy hours,
barks at the infidels, growls at the kids,
is a model mammal, imperfect but steadfast,
knows full tilt grind and nothing more,
is driven, yes, but pure.

From moon to moon, sun to sun,
19 endures the ten thousand violences.
Here is 19's day:
He awakes 4:30 a.m. to the blaring alarm.   He has slept
badly to a neighbor's bass beat and 3am honking.   His wife
stirs to make breakfast – he says no and sloughs off to the
diner where he eats the wrong order to a yelling couple
and is charged with a smile ten times the cost of the food.
He swerves an hour through hypoglycemic traffic and
arrives at the worksite ten minutes late where he's greeted
by the boss with a requisite sneer.   He spends the morning
with cheap nails and lumber for a cheap, pretty structure
that he will never enter.   Lunch is fine but for the long
line and indolent food cart guy.   He returns to find his
hammer stolen.   He borrows one from the smiling co-

worker who stole it. Same nails and wood. Same hours.
Same structure. At day's end he asks for his late check and
receives a lie with a smile. On the ride home he receives
a death stare from a fervent yuppie. He slams brakes for
a woman crossing against traffic and receives a fuck you.
He can't find a full parking space and has to walk the last
three blocks home. He loves his squabbling kids to the
ends of the earth. His tired wife has made a lovely frugal
meal. They curl up to bad news and sarcastic jokes. He
drifts to diligent sleep to a neighbor's bass beat. The ten
thousand violences seep through his skin like toxins.

The sun beats.
The crust cracks.
Scree skitters.
The pond grows thin.
19 succumbs.
Gulls scatter.
A cry goes up —

not for one man but for the home itself,
for 19 is cornerstone, tap root, well spring, and when
sockdolager rots the marrow, snaps the bearing beam
the jaw cannot chew,
the loss of blood is too great,
the estuary dries,

the amphibians drag themselves onto the plain
to desiccate, to bare the spine,
fluids leached into soil,
the frank flexibility of bone denied.

And so the comitatos flies,
the ants desert, knowing
the brief space of life
and the vast engine
of conflict and love, a mute
ending and a frank song starting.

THE SONG OF REARING

The spine rears
> *and a rose blooms.*

The ire rears
> *and the sea shines.*

The iron rears
> *and the hands open.*

The clime rears
    and an engine roars.

The sanctum rears
    and the veils drop.

The callous rears
    and men walk abroad.

The shank rears
    and the home is built.

The rose rears
    and a tone sounds.

The face rears
    and a mountain shifts.

The grin rears
    and a tree buds.

The posse rears
    and the spine reveals.

EDENTULOUS FANTASY

Lying on concrete
champing bare gums
reaching for sockets' memory,
I think of (of all things) galaxies and rocks,
of the matter that con-cerns us —
dirt, plants, respite, meat, the food of
burning, recalcitrant gluck,
the final muck that brings us home
to stalk the metal, glass, and flesh of
this breath, this shine, even this
white grit belying the evanescent task
of eating rock, teething on jade, of
churning the weather of the heart
in this great maw.

Shelterless, thirty-two soldiers huddle
stamping and chattering in the night,
while the earth spins and a hundred billion stars
burn effortlessly. All about the chill vast
sense of space. Slowly it dawns
on them that they mayn't have

made it across the border,
mayn't have made it
at all.

Shalom, shalom,
empty cork, empty bone;
receive, receive
in the breach, in the eve.

I line my new toothbrush with paste
and plunge it in to scrub
nothing, I have
forgotten, cavern deep and echoing
the chanting of teeth alone —
I don't know what I am,
and the ghosts still haunt the empty gum,
asking for movement, shift, a shock
of new weather, blast of amnesty, new river,
an undertow to rip them from
this tide of fucked-up woe, alas,
and toss them to the strafing wind
that sweeps the desert clean.

Has the toothless man nothing but memory? No. He has
the ordnance of memory.
Deep in the hills, a cache of tiny capsules lies in wait,
guarding the human sap for the mindful rearing.
Each holds the pudding of a mighty race
concentrated into joy and crouching will.
You hold the talisman within your face,
and say the word, and watch the passion spill.

Salaam, salaam,
the dead can help you;
believe, believe
a wave, a call.

A castle, a cathedral
empty, full
holes within holes
substantive, practical
lacunae
in a structure
that cannot be without
space, loss

founding a pillar
lingering, ghosts
shaping the keystone
reeds, our lives
shorn and reprieved
again and again
we recognize the fading leaf
for what we lose, we gain,
and what we keep, we loose into the rain.

What happens when appearances are gone?
The ghost no longer gives a shit.
That is the secret of rearing.
The rear is more threatening than the splay.
The rear entices where the splay ignores.
The rear provokes. The rear jeers.
The rear shows its belly – if only to you.

Ubiquitous, ubiquitous,
guilty and loving;
call to me, call to me
and I arrive.

And you plod on, crunching underfoot
a molar, gravel, dirty ice,
a set of rings, a thigh bone, shattered
city, millennia, the leaking
atmosphere *wham* in the belly
and you're thrown, drifting
       who knows why
          a pattern of
        reluctance
    withholding
        thin air
           until
      the rearing
    the rear becomes apparent
spine arched in space   the nerves
      so full of rock   biding
          cauterize
     absence to a root
          shirk the sheer enamel
      seek the lurking pulp
           raise the dormant sprite
          and catalyze
       a breed of gnashers roaring in the night.

Tooth of Grieving

30 – Lower Right 1ˢᵗ Molar

What lives
after so much fury?
What gives the tornado
after the blow?
After so much, what gives?
The poor dwarf stands before the altar,
hands fluttering at his sides,
face numb, brow frozen
by the lash, lips set
to be stung again,
one choice in mind:
to stand, remain, bide
against the rain,
stone tower,
storm shutter,
iron fence,
secret barbary of indifference,
secret frame of reference....

30, 19's twin, is first to look out
the window into the egregious dew-soaked
hour stretching to days
and a breath comes in
and does not leave
until the sated sight relieves itself
in gasping seizures on the floorboards
pure grief fluid from the face
gasping fluid spasms for all the beauty
joy wonder and amazing fucking shit
gone from 19 gone gasping lost
he will not be lifted from his chair
he will not share a deeply honored toast
he will not well at the sight of a single grin
gone fucking lost
and a breath comes in, goes out
scenting the blood of dew and
30's sympathetic root starts to stop
shaking, bashing little walls and
shuddering about the question.

The heart and lungs cry out
and the teeth taste of antibodies.

30 is heartfelt but
cold and sick,
at the end of his
weathered rope,
takes desperate measures,
wraps himself in plastic
for a little warmth
sense of touch
little pocket of heat
lays there panting
for ages
conserving
preserving
trying to
remain
needs a little
rock
finally
wraps himself in earth
so smooth and welcoming
restorative
familiar
finely beaten
warm.

19's twin holds the fort,
flexes hands, takes time,
takes refuge in the meticulous
regaining, in
measuring the store and
preparing once again to care,
and sets about the work of keeping
the staves strong, staving off frost,
and saving breath for the structure.
Each breath measured, each breath steeled
with the tenacity of the battered,
solemnity of the damned,
deep recognition,
stark refusal,
rage with a kernel of scar.

The heart and lungs cry out

What shall I eat tonight, tonight,
what shall I eat tonight
when all of my wrongs are right, are right
and the cat has stolen my might?

And yes, the cat sits in a corner
tweakling with the last of the molars,
batting about and sundrying
and casting doubt on the meal.

There is a general feeling of fright for the weakest conduit.

Tooth of Masks

3 – Upper Right 1ˢᵗ Molar

One big mouth a
fool of fun with an
emaciated tooth with a
coat of gold and a
sculpted past on a
bench of fear, singing
   Cha cha cha cha!
   Re-envision!

Dance of metal, spring lad
laughing all the way to the
slab — eternal smooth
like nothing you've ever
hid behind — just an overlay
just a singlet just a
   Cha cha cha!

Sought after, flung after
without comprehension,

such a smooth ride
tinkling the shiny keys of your
vaulted cave, yummy as copper,
bloody as bonds, the godawful godlike chin
towers above   you   mewling
pandering and denigrating thy
self   head   throat   lips and all
all for a li'l nip of
                    Cha cha cha cha!
a mistaken identity
an identity mistook
sweet smooth metal your cells
calling for an old clay friend
and finding a smiley penny.

Who is that masked tooth?
                    cha cha

Sometimes a tragic thrust
mates the right cast of mettle
for a grit that springs
innovation from the dusk,
gathers grains and plans
livestock games and history

builds a strategic sublevel
inviolate subterfugal
safety croon bone tender
cave of *cha cha cha*
a dense survival
by invitation only.

What spire rises from the lair
to show its fierce mask?

       Cha   cha cha

Another combination
or recombinant invention
crafts a catapult and cape
burgeoning strata and erstwhile angst
joining the winds of justice
with a catalytic chant

       Cha cha cha cha!
       Re-collision!

up up and earnest
behind the crafty cloak
soars a singular streak
into stark contest
cannot be altered

even as the skirmish
rips layer from layer of
you guessed it

cha cha cha cha cha cha

challenging maleficence
with force of mimicry
appearing and appearing
two teeth twelve eyes the face of a loon
shocking fur furious tusks a roar of
tendrils tentacles and huge blooms
the steady stream of face-in-face
effacing the opponent
and the blunt shift revealing.

Tournied and ravaged
3 won't leave the party,
sips on a chai,
has a little chit-chat,
succumbs to the endemic flaw
with an occasional mind-ploy,
slips back to the dance floor
to work it all out
with a wild little skillful little

Cha cha cha cha!

while the band wails
>
> *Cha cha cha!*
> *Re-incision!*
> *Re-decision!*
> *Re-division!*
> *Re-revision!*
> *Re-re-*RE-RE-RE-RE-RE-RE-RE-RE

Tooth of Endurance

9 – Upper Left 1ˢᵗ Incisor

Delight keeps the old man spry.
Lovely perseverant, take the rent with
a sweep of sheen — How gracious
the year mere as lightning
shocked and shot, the first, the
fleetest runner pardoned for backward
roots by the seem seam — lovely trickle
of shorn shards and cored
undulation, carved, stunned,
struck and honored — first, fleetest,
finest — beeline dancer, darting
spree, sheer scirocco
settled into reverence and, rightly, you,
Old Man on a Stick,
you do rock the house, keep the raft afloat,
burgeon more than mere mortality.

tck - a - ch   tck - a - ch
tck - a - tck - a - tu - ch

Fleetest run now farthest trod,
it is for your seeming frictionlessness
that you are honored.
On and on, Old Man, still
on the long wave, glidin' long and
you know the weather, don't you —
mum and murk, wild and wide-tired,
tried and truncated, wrinkled, treacled —
gorgeous as a star glidin' long
through a smooth combustion,
you do not strain, do not bog,
and knowing is the heart of it,
the prime beat and burn
rocking the cantankerous day in its crib.
All along you've streamed
and streaming is your shine —
peaks will rise, god love 'em,
birds will drop from the sky,
behemoths will trundle in your path,
yet you, rocking chair, triathlete,
you know the water on your back and bask,
glide, stream on, you know the trick
of being water for an instant.

tck - a - tck - a - tu - ch
tck - a - tck - a - tu - ch

What sparked this water-off-back
effortlessness? Easy. Much water on back.
You were dealt a hand and a half, weren't you,
wrong color, wrong suit, wrong set of cards,
all rotten, cursed, malifluent,
and in the cataract you stood, and soared,
each drop a petal, each obstacle a grace,
each son-bitch an ally in the night.
It is not a how, as some expect, but
a wherefore, a lightship generated
by your wings, fleetest, swooping
through brick, through blight,
through the taunt-blown streets. Delight keeps
the old man spry, slicing through life
with a reverence that shines beyond
his own recognizance,
and though he pays a price for all this
touchlessness, this wearing of the skin,
though he glides on a vacuum about and within,
enameled and deprived —

storm-dancer, slam-surfer —
his light strides ringing and clear
through the harking crowd drawn
to his fortitude, his reverence,
delight reflects and drenches him,
repelled, repelled again, amplifying
and compelling them to awe, propelling him
into a charge that lifts arms eyes face spine
hobble and all, lifts them all into life,
strife gone, the dance begun,
community in act,
the body kept.

tck - a - tck   tck - a - tck - a
tck - a - tck   tck - a - tck - a

9's song is an allegro tap staccato
stick-tapped in a rat-trap rage,
that flings him from the body cage,
leaves strain assuaged, shine engaged, and everyone amazed
because song is mind, and that is 9's mind.

tck - a - ch   tck - a - ch   tck - a - tck - a - tu - ch
tck - a - ch   tck - a - ch   tck - a - tck - a - tu - ch
tck - a - tck - a - tu - ch   tck - a - tck - a - tu - ch
tck - a - tck   tck - a - tck - a   tck - a - tck   tck - a - tck - a
tck - a - CH   tck - a - tck - a - tck - a - CH   tck - a - tck - a
    - tck - a - CH
tck - a - tck - a - tck - a - tu - CH   tck - a - tck - a - tck - a -
    tu - CH - ck -
tck - a - tck - a - tck - a - tu - CH - ck - tck - a - tck
tck - a - CH - ck - tck - a - tck - a - tck - a - tu - CH - ck - tck -
    a - tck
tck - a - ch   tck - a - ch   tck - a - tck - a - tu - ch
tck - a - ch   tck - a - ch   tck - a - tck - a - tu - ch
tck - a - CH   tck - a - tck - a - tck - a - CH - ck - tck - a - tck
tck - a - CH   tck - a - tck - a - tck - a - CH - ck - tck - a - tck
tck - a - tck   tck - a - tck - a   tck - a - tck   tck - a - tck - a
tck - a - tck   tck - a - tck - a   tck - a - tck   tck - a - tck - a
tck - a - tck   tck - a - tck - a   tck - a - tck   tck - a - tck - a
tck - a - tu - CH.

That stick is the fastest frickin' thing around.

Tooth of Anger

24 – Lower Left 1ˢᵀ Incisor

There is no *Grrrrr* like a tooth *grrrrr*.
The comedy of anger pleats the palate
with a soft grin that rides
your marrow like a stamen
ready to spew. Chuckling we
bury the hatchet with a song —

Forehead throbs, and out bobs a
canine, playtime, rapine
ready for the Pharaoh
consequence is narrow

— while on and on the hatchet lies
ready, tucked between the hemispheres
like a rogue incisor. 24
pretends to show, to magnanimously
grant grace, proffer aid,
and wish a prosperous crop

profusely, but hides deftly (even from itself)
the bristling spines that live to prick,
a blind collusion and a plan to wreak
a nation of its own becoming,
tsunami of its all-consuming rave,
a nation whose masses eat themselves.

24 thinks itself a cleaver,
slicer, partisan,
Scythe of Ages, Super-Knife,
a scimitar of righteous wrath,
posse, cavalry, comitatos, surgeon,
returner of all undeservéd strife,
but in truth grinds and grinds away
at the forceps of conflict,
must mosh, slam, foster clash,
bash its neighbors strong and lame,
shameless and oblivious,
has a vein running right through the pulp
pulling blood that you need into dark rot,
into a sliver of chipped blade waiting
to slice again, eager
to maim the fiend, shaking
with flared brute brilliance.

Each rush of air
through sharp nostrils
makes the heart keener,
the brow ripped wide.

Forehead, forehead, kamikaze sure did
fit in a split and shit on a nitwit
bored red boar-head rama laissez-faire head
knitting a fine line deadline Mordred

When 24 is very smart,
it is a fuse for pain and genesis,
it dives the razor river, rides
the mad horse through the streets of yes,
chides the insolent and surfs its way
into a catalytic palimpsest of town
wherein compassion is the architect,
frustration fuels the masonry,
and malice feeds the cattle by the stream —
it streams the scream into a lovelorn song
that chances all for sake of clearing ground,

gathers everyone around to flail
obduration in a drumbeat spree,
leaves destruction for an act of spring,
chews through the chicken-wire
to a yard full of sunshine
and dances the big dances the big we.

But when 24 burns,
its fuse has just one end,
the ending of itself by nighting mind
and catapulting reason for the bye-bye rage
of a giant child launching flaming
body-bludgeon-cannon-teeth
to cleanse the stained horizon
and hurl the rank repulsive one to death, death, death —
it burns with the fission of a city,
whole blocks shorn to dust,
whole men muted to molten sand,
cracked crust, calcic scree,
integrity of the continent compromised,
bedrock of the plate rent.
24 becomes a mask of flesh,
a sheath of hate, a crown of force,
a wide, wide mouth with no remorse.

Forehead splits and out spits a
snakemind, de-fined, red lined
eye becomes a shotgun
poised for a blood run
bullride shared
for a load of
fun

Tooth of Alert

8 – Upper Right 1ˢᵗ Incisor

An eye drifting sharply;
a mind on point;
a keen watch; a vigil;
a padmasana.

8 watches the pin drop,
finds a tiny egg beneath your thumb,
smells sand over the ridge,
hears singing days in advance.
Such talent! or vitality.

Creep on over the grassy dune,
brow arched, fingers bold, lips stretched
above a glint of grin — ready to flip
spin and shimmy
                through the arching day
the ringing scent of rain
ushering you to your next *balancez*.

What kind of warrior are you, 8?

unbeholden

The senses live unhoused
in the meteoric spree
of candles, ice, and battered horns,
flacked by shards and churning nails,
pinions of duress flocking
through a wilderness of
ranting num-chuck roil
to a single stainless stanchion
from which vantage is revealed.

8 hops on a mountain bike
and tears through the streets
blazing
— we have known this man —
dancing with traffic
threading his flesh through
bricks, metal, mirrors, hunks of glass
each absolutely known, smelled
quantified
dodging solids
howling through canyons
sieving air.

So many addled,
so many moments lost to the
blur of the carousel,
so many purblind to the
falling rock, the hail,
perturbations, mass migrations,
their own fumblings and flailings,
knocking over the teacup, draining the well,
so many simply slicing
without knowing that they slice,
— we have seen them —
crouching over the world,
worried over tissue, grass, pebbles,
        lost glasses,
a toy tossed   over the roof
— we have been them —
crazy magnets, easy targets,
collateral,
lightning rods.

8 keeps a sheer eye
sees the splay and rear
sees all 32 in a flash
gathers without touching

has no interest in clash
only in being allowed to live
— this woman is in our home —
stands mid-ridge
allows movement
allows the flailing of grief and joy
lies flat on the floor
rings a bell in each corner
sings to the remaining teeth
      calling blood
      calling bone
      calling solid ground.

What do you think you're doing, 8?

You park a fractured horse and disrobe
the chicken-wire world.
You wield the charcoal stick of stealth
and scratch home, scratch home.
You churn a cauldron of liberty,
and spill it on the floor.
All this and why?

8 wishes only
a few moments where he may have fish.

Alert the tiny socket
Alert the jolting spree
Alert the fierce hen in a storm
Alert the bottom egg in a barrel
Alert cats in a library
Alert you in a cage
Alert the hair on end
Alert between the eyes
Alert the towering oak
Alert the dry grasses
Alert, yes, the lightning rod
Alert the wind, always the wind
whose sigh is 8's song:

shhhhhh
shhh shhhhh
shhhhhhhhhhhhhhhhhhhhhhhhhhhhhhhhhhhhhhhh

Tooth of Inspiration

#25 – Lower Right 1st Incisor

25 breathes,
as you might expect.
Born veiled,
she is charged to minister her kind,
to gently part the newborn's caul,
breathe in the fresh face, breathe with,
whirl in and out with the absolute
spouting from the edifice.

25 drinks her world straight up.

Five fives dance around
flinging "Eat me! Eat me!" to the stars,
"We are four fours and a nine
or whatever the lava unbars!"

We take what the what the fuck
over the hill under the lime through the
everlovin bramble-ridden full gale into the
clear blue profit-sacked self-cleaning

ardent indifferent we bang it up
you fix it self-contained remunerated panoply
proffers, and what we do with it
face in the wind don't hold your breath
let the dogs out take your clothes off
charge up the roll down the cut the twine
let the full-blown wind of dawn steal your
dive in the river ride the ringing tearing
caterwauling unlicensed fool
takes us.

Five fives take a ride
under the beaming faucet bridge
where kneecaps dive and doggies writhe
and time learns how to give.

She harrows the world with a spade of flesh
to gather the senses to a spot honed
for being; adores the debris that whispers of
tiny movements, shifts of naming, of empathies,
presents cataclysm and storm, relics and gifts;
stands amidst with arms spread breathing;
allows herself to know when to move;
darts from touching to touching;
takes in the altered earth of civilization;

reaps the product from the shelves;
strokes the sleek pounded metal of cars;
parts the politician's grin;
welcomes the unscripted body;
rips the paper from the pecker;
holds a mirror to your face;
loosens that which lies and has lain
for ages into the sweet breeze;
and lets the teem tell its own tale
in naked tongues in the bright bright night.

Five fives bounce around
a floorless roofless wallless room
filling with light and frogs until they
boom boom boom.

25 loves apocalypse
as a pristine delicacy
waiting to be recognized,
the big surprise that bides beneath the tooth,
yet does not seek it
or seeks only as she breathes,
for seeking is dependent on the sought
and corrupts as dank desire will,
while breathing is autonomic,

an autonomy of rock,
of thrusting hail, allowing,
auto-nomic, self-law.

Five fives present themselves
a lavish fountain in the fog
gushing an undulating gnash
that dreamers find unshod.

To unveil the unveiling
is not an inspired act
in itself; rather the manner
of inhalation
re-acts, releasing the golden threads
to huff life back to the twitching hands,
to chime the cells with repartee,
to light the thalamus from within,
to raise consonance in the body,
in the concentric living day.

Five fives release themselves
into the ratcheting soup of glee
and sheerly snakely make a pretty
racket of what could be.

You walk down the street breathing,
smiling, looking through air when
something puts a hand through your brow,
another through your chest, gently tugs,
you slide out through arms into sanctity,
and humbly you are 25, lower right first incisor,
five fives, veil-born, chipped digger,
sentient vertebrate, giver of things,
breather of faces, letter of many leaves,
utterly you in the panoptic sanguine
gift of you they we.

Tooth of Order

#10 – Upper Left 2ND Incisor

10 is a mechanic, works hard,
pays taxes, follows sports,
goes to church and town meetings,
helps the needy, suffers the fool,
believes in God, country,
and following the law.

For once, a normal tooth.

Stolid 10 lives in a machine
called the world, a land constructed
by the iron hand of right that sternly
lovingly places cogs and braces
staves against the storm, curses chance
and the brute brunt of time.

Awed! Awed! and borne
by the track, by the vectored mind
seeking a little peace in
structure, in
the measured line.

10 fights the fracturing pinions
that torque the ubiquitous wheel,
must harness insidious water in every form
(freeze, rust, and rot are not for him!),
mounts floodlights against the creeping
tenebrous failure of the eye,
wrestles the ruinous angel of stress
with every thought, with every breath.

Let us pray
that today
will allay
decay.

10 sees the future as a great blob,
hungry, monotonous, tamed,
a panoply of homogeny surely
safely marching toward the autumn
of corruption and the poor confuséd throng
where a cleansing blast awaits,
where cities craft' of sand
harbor gentle folk from hail and lash
and break through form into decorous
plinths and friezes, captivating

mind-formations born of noble truths
and goodness, virtue, valor,
freedom, blah, equality,
and, well, you know what I mean.
In the glaring arc of the welding torch
his eyes burn
with the stamp and boom of its generation.

Awed! Awed! and stultified
by treacle and the reasoned rhyme,
comfortably caged in
credence in
the arch of time.

10 corrects grammar, by the way. Constantly.
It drives his co-workers crazy.
They understand each other just fine,
and understand that the language is well.
Bottom line is, 10 likes to stay on top of things.
It makes him feel, well, on top of things.

10 is a tooth
because he says he is.

10 thinks competition is a healthy thing,
builds character (sorry about that ear!),
puts a neat perspective on the chaos
of the rearing world, and, best of all,
gives one the chance to quantify one's prowess,
to canter for the fans,
shows da bums who's the man.

Yee-haw!
Gimme the ball!
Watch me brawl!
Hiya, Ma!

10 likes hearing his name in the lists,
likes this poem quite a bit, in fact,
though it is a bit, er, obtuse,
and maybe not the part about the hand.
Goddamn poets.

Awed! Awed! and shorn
by the die, by the sand hand
drifting up the vertebrae
to settle in
the living strand.

10 has one recurring nightmare.
A cracked hand rises from the ashpot,
palm cracked down the centerline,
says nothing,
shows, in fact, indifference.
The flesh parts (silently),
the bones reveal themselves
and start to laugh,
joints clacking and chuckling,
then clatter to the floor in a jumbled heap.
Nothing neat about it.

Forsooth
such a tooth
knows the truth
sans ruth.

For all his quirks, for all his
qualms and quantifying, quibbling, quips,
and quagmires, he brings a welcomed
certainty to the melee,
a stricture to the hectic jaw.
For all his careful framing, for all his
bright lights, poor meticulous 10
cannot see
a small animal scurrying in the dark wood.

Tooth of Discernment

23 – Lower Left 2ND Incisor

23 wanders through the woods after an ice storm,
seeing every branch, each sprig coated in gleaming glass.
It is early spring and there are buds enshrined,
each new twig has its aim, each branch its weight,
each trunk its stock. Even the new grass,
pushing through the crust, respires, each blade
illumined, reified, awesome, lush.
Her boots crunch loudly and she stops to hear the hush
broken by a drip here and a crack there,
the smacking of boughs in the breeze,
the tinkling crash of tiny ice-falls,
the stir of small life, and the scent of freeze.
No detail escapes — a mottled bark, encrusted moss,
a young fern splayed, each magnified
by light and fog slowly rising into the brightening sky.
23 listens to the lifting mist and lets a soft sound,
louder than breath but quieter than a palpable sigh.

Let her sing branches anew, anew,
let her tumble into the ever-grown hay.
Find her a creature that she may show,
and sing children's terrors away.

Traveller, farer, journeyer,
thine eye rends sameness
and touches the exclusive
track of being. You caress
objects like they've never been,
make them be, and let them drift
into the next countenance.
Create the simple stillness for us,
and retract our ever-sated eye.
Let us see again, so we may be
as the wind which culminates the day.

Let her blow through the imagined land,
give her a steady bearing and a vantage to claim.
Let her sit quietly by the shore
and give the horizon a name.

The wilderness rises to greet her: bricks and stone rise,
old milk jugs, automobiles rise, faces of salesmen,
architects, hypocrites rise, the new sun rises,
cantilevers, furnaces, pixels rise, all types of
cheekbones, irises, derma rise, weddings rise,
parades rise, bombs and daggers rise, leaves
and tomes and old shells rise, the veins
of the leaves rise, lines of the tomes rise, faintly
tinted ridges of the shells rise, she sees them all
rise and mingle, palpitate, remix,
shift and struggle, yes, vie, prevaricate,
dominate, repress, endure great pain,
spit and deceive, prosper, soar,
countless parts and things, incantatory, real,
displayed each with its valued features
all on an even plain.

And let her be a siren and let her be a star,
and let her pour into the world,
and let her be clear as the eye of the storm,
and let her see things as they are.

23 walks through the town she has lived many years
and sees the strange turns of brick, of cornice,
mysterious inscriptions on the founding stones,
layers of road, repainted signs,
the transportation of goods, services enacted,
doors opened, greetings made true and untrue,
and faces, faces seen and never seen,
a different one sad now, a new one revered,
a momentary shock on that, an infant in the air,
a lined one with another cause, an apoplectic girl,
a battered jinn, a spurned chanteuse, a comet and a tail,
each with specific eyes, a turn of lip, a curve of ear,
hair unlike else, a brow defined as if seen under ice
for a moment, waiting to churn, to splice,
to blend and propagate,
all buds, the new road, the year.

Let her bring trinkets afar, afar,
let her congregate with the finest of clans.
Let her touch every kind of hair
and marvel in every strand.

And with thine eye you register,
measure, take a step, open palms,
lift the veils, recognize, embrace the weak
and strong in each, flaws and talents one, and know
fear from a hole in the ground,
fashion from despair,
color from deception,
fantasy from grace,
peace from war.

And let her be a siren and let her be a star,
and let her pour into the world,
and let her be clear as the eye of the storm,
and let her see things as they are.

When 23 straps on her pack, purely stocked
with air and eye only, no need for camera or knife,
when she canters, takes her leave,
you may pang, may want, but you should not,
for though she will voyage, in one sense, and sense it is,
her journey is optic, she is rooted in light,
she can visit without ever moving,
and in the split of a grin
she sees you.

TOOTH OF EMPATHY

#7 – UPPER RIGHT 2ND INCISOR

7 turns onto Main Street,
pulls over, gets out,
and lies in the middle of the road
face down, smelling old tar and road dust.
He's driven long and hard to find
this spot, this smell, and suddenly
everyone in town catches an unexplained
whiff of tar. And he lays there
slowly, calmly catching
turkey breast, motor oil, cans,
window cleaner, old rope, sweat,
dogshit, cheesefries, fresh mown grass,
bandaids, bleach, spaghetti sauce, shoe polish,
chocolate, hair spray, several brands of car exhaust,
old leaves, cut wood, cheap perfume, lip balm,
moth balls, wet shoes, fresh paint, mink oil,
linseed oil, olive oil, baby oil, lighter fluid,
dry cleaning, cheap scotch, and candles.
And he knows the rest are there as well.

la la la   la la la

We all know the moon pulls the tide,
but how does the shore sing to the gulls?
The earth meets the mouth in tiny slides
of plant and nerve and parching soil.
The breached gum parting meets its match
in the tweaking tendons of the jaw.
The smile shifts, cheeks drift, reeds stir,
and somewhere in the air a gull cries back.
And still, the candles.

la la lay, la lie

Whelmed by the moment, each citizen begins
a new stride of thought in the afternoon:
one drops her bills to write a postcard,
one starts a new crochet,
a cribbage game breaks up
in favor of a front porch kibbutz,

a mechanic sets down his tools
for a walk in the park,
an old woman cuts short her morning stroll
to call on a long-missed friend,
a fisherman throws back his catch
and sits on the dock with his feet in the lake....

la la low, lay lie

How do men conceive an island
they inhabit? As a whole.
One must smell the dense groves,
the salt-strafed beaches, the gloaming
of dells that have forgotten
plummeting rock, the human step,
the ache of erosion.
This isle is no isle
without each new leaf, each
hunk of trash, each cracked façade,
each scent of metal and of flame,
and a hungry fen with a gap-toothed grin.

la la low   low   low

Drifting in scent, the man
becomes a raven plunging
in a steep survival dive, a baby
surging in mid-birth, a field
of wild daisies thriving, a rich
miasma percolating all the earth's things.
He flutters into air, feels grit beneath,
hard road, eyes flutter open,
rises on one elbow, and finds himself mid-road
surrounded by a shocked melee.
One man steps forward (reeking of cheap cologne)
and asks, officious yet concerned,
"Are you ok?"

la la lay, la la lie,
la la lay, la la lie lie,
la la low, la lay,
lie, lie.

And everywhere about, these sounds
leak from the earth like a happy fen
full of dancing new things making
even more new things making even more.
O the poor man who shuns the fen.

Tooth of Nurturing

26 – Lower Right 2ND Incisor

Plant and weave, plant and weave,
scent of soil, scent of thread,
the hand that looms and sifts the loam
will settle lightly on your head.

The hand plants seeds
as it has for centuries
this is not a new tale
but a compelling one yes
for in it lies your flesh.
It is not the motion
dig and turn, furrow and drop
that is the planting
scratch and cleave, hollow and spill
but the measure of seed and soil
with the eye, with the hand
an acuity of every sense
the sifting, the holding
not the motion but the measure
rapidly, rapidly

in the parting touch of fingers
instilling, releasing
almost a caressing snap
tasting, delving
in the knowledge of the flesh
the earth is ripe, the furrow fresh,
the seed receives its kind.

26 steps outside
and sinks into a womb.

The hand weaves strands
of sand, of silk, of spectacle
with pigment from the living mouth,
the meat of cells, heat of the brain patiently
breathing tones to shelter, brighten
the difficult day with a simple tug
of fiber, slide of wool, motion of the mind
looming actively, a spool springing anima
to a hook threading potent to an
eye meshing a calm rill
in a sheet of fine.
The fabric stretches out, spills
across the room in waves bounding

ages and causeways
leasing into flesh the wind of
ancestors, erudition, twining
history to a cloak, memory to a tapestry,
a woven cask, a wicker mat, a quilt of
handshakes, dawnings, broken dreams,
fields of passion, sharp mementos,
aspirations, stone retreats,
and songs to soothe the bitter wind.

26 wraps the world in flesh,
wraps flesh in the world.

The hand plants teeth
as reminders, as remedial
an ancient custom
founding, fundamental
a pruning of sorts
to loose the pannier of loss
and prime the loam for tendrils
of a new receive,
to cultivate a life regained.
Bone goes to earth
under biding mounds

shaped and released
a year recedes
churning, dreaming
and hillocks turn to heartbeats
liminal, thrumming
calling sparrows and mice
to burrow, to nest
a refuge secured
to bring seeds, to perform
and a forest is born
flourishing, burgeoning
full of birdcall.

26 puts in the ground
just what needs to return.

The hand weaves sounds
to lift the heart from clay,
to barn dance with the loving throng that
tumbles from the molten shale and into
the crucible of fusion and decay,
to resonate the chambers of the marl.
Music slides off her fingers like rain
soaking the nerves with a salve of

soil, the globe itself freshening the blood
through her fingers a salient stream of
nutrient. You stand planted
in a new-found wood, breathing in the musk of green
and bark. The golden sun drips on your face and
grass grows through your feet. A pattern of leaves
flutters right through you. Step out into the day.

26 is so in love
her face comes off.

The body plants, the body weaves
scent of marrow, scent of song,
the arms that lift and shuttle you
will bring the living world along.

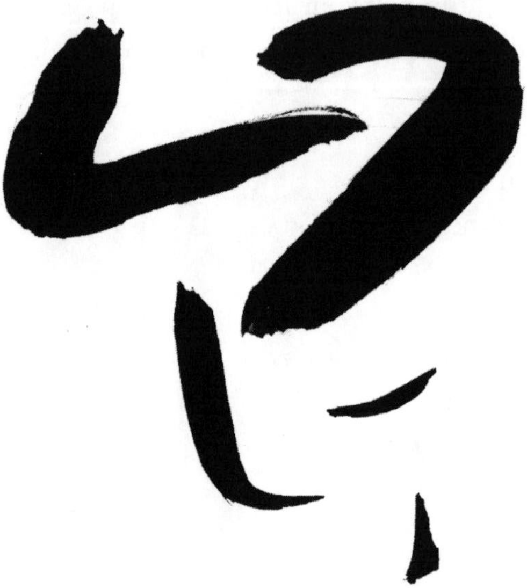

TOOTH OF SEX

#11 – UPPER LEFT CANINE

11 is my gay tooth.
It holds all my gay powers:
walking down the street,
drinking water,
looking through windows,
putting on a t-shirt,
dialing the phone,
shifting my weight in a chair,
stepping out of a car,
standing on a boulder in the woods,
yelling at the top of my lungs,
pouring a cup of coffee,
smelling a pepper stew,
darting a glance,
putting clothes in the dryer,
wrapping silk around my head,
lying on the roof on a sunny afternoon,
lying face down in the grass,
sucking on a lemon,
sucking on ice,
licking an envelope,

smelling fall leaves,
twisting around to kiss you,
rolling in feathers,
rolling in mud,
climbing a tree,
opening my eyes upon waking,
stretching full yawn,
touching my toe to carpet,
resting my foot on your thigh,
standing in rain,
blowing bubbles,
watching a fire,
frying sweet onions,
spinning around and around,
tracing your jaw with my fingertip,
hovering over your breast,
lifting you into the air,
and allowing myself to be lifted.

Not necessarily in that order.

OK, so maybe 11 isn't *strictly* gay.
11 don't need the *cat*egory,
catty, just smells what's good

and knows it when nipples pop,
groin throbs, and all the doors open.
11 leans in the dark to 10's ear
and asks, close and sexy,
What are you wearing?

11 wants
to get every fluid moving
this has always happened, it is good
to mesh flesh
for every minute message of the orb
to feel no difference (for a second)
the protozoan gathers
thrusting forward
chromosomes tense
the merge of nerve, curve of the arm
incipient forms emerge
soft hide of the instep, heave of the chest
spindles align
tolling of cells, of midriff shift
organelles riffing
affection mirror, caution stripper
salt bringer, neuralgic life cleaner
nerves honed, pristine, in contact
start to stream

your flesh in my mouth
membranes dissolve
my flesh in your warm wet silken
urgent pull of
limbs, fingers, saliva, sweat, funk
primal leap to
nipples rolling in lips
remember copper and mushrooms
ripping loose
whole skin unbridled
writhing, sliding
bliss gaping
satiated throb
between two worlds
surging
to cry out, to join a
metasynaptic
third —
to lapse, disperse, to drift
a final kiss
to form and separate
to linger in the scent of your nape
to breathe ourselves clean
to breathe and be breathed
to be very alive.

11 sings a low low moan
inside you every day,
with everything you do
a syncopating tone
rings deep in the bone,
resonating cell to cell,
till all your tissues undulate
primeval charge, harmonic humm
saturating, coursing veins
limbs chest guts sex bolting
up the spine through your skull
radiating lovingly
out every hole you have.

Tooth of Exhibition

#22 – Lower Left Canine

The beat at the heart of a tooth
is the beat of a radiant wing
lifting the thrum of a vibrant drum
to a mind of fire and pearl.

22 is the stress of a bird flying with the wind
manifest in an 86-year-old showgirl —
weathered, petulant, lives to play,
stores every frill of finesse and folderol
within arms' reach – sings a song of
seabreeze to herself every morning,
a shadow shanty to her other self at night.

Hey breeze, hey sunny beam,
bring me a golden egg,
hunt me a fairing eye
and shine, shine

Please, hey seas,
spin me a silken tide,
throw me a shiny stone
so rare, rare

She breaks her fast with an Irish tea,
a dusting of chestnut rouge,
iridescent eye shadow (sky today),
brand new lashes,
lip gloss to part the seas,
seven molecules of ambergris,
and a side of whole wheat toast.

Breeze, hey breeze,
rear me a cheery mare,
carry me safe inside
this day dream life

Duty done, she turns to the task
of summoning her moxie.
This she can accomplish in a number of ways.

She may take a stroll through the garden,
or jump up and down making monkey sounds.
She may breathe and stretch, warble and spin,
or just stand at the window and drink it all in.
Thus staged, and made, and cauldron warm,
she opens the door and begins to perform.

This ain't just any old tooth, girl —
she takes her day by *storm* —
boogies on down to the bo-de-ga,
fox trots out to the fair,
switches back to the laund-dro-mat,
hops on the bus, hops on the bus,
stomps on the pavement, struts in the square,
shimmies downtown for a spell,
spins in the tap room, swings in the spotlight,
ho - ay - oh, ho - ay - oh —
No foolin — she takes a big cherry to her lips
and riffs the archetype —
hair whips out to string you up
tenderly, red smoke rises from her tits,
and that sly ol' smile shines right through,
glinting, revving, ready to rip —

This girl is *packed*, she rides the rumbleseat
with mambo thighs, she wields a
wild eye, she kicks a heel
through the ceiling, she gots jazz
leakin from her anus. We're talkin *body*.
We're talkin *spine*. And in the big of the night,
blazing all bells,
what rivets her to life is riveting
the howling throng to a truck o' joy —
borne to calliope, born to spark a tune
down to the last coda,
to the last shorn wing.

How she pleases.
How she pulls a rug, rubs an eye,
bows out.

Goodnight, little light,
hallow night and beam well,
Farewell, little bell,
you shadow-ring, shadow-ring,

Goodnight, little bird,
may the wind be your friend
and nestle you into
the end, the end.

TOOTH OF REBELLION

#6 – UPPER RIGHT CANINE

Raucous, naughty, must have shift
flicking tonguing
torch and pitchfork —
write a ticket kick the lava
smite a hypocrite and live
fling a llama shave a doctor
sting a hoochie-coochie proctor
love a lobster rub a mobster
let saliva loose — goose everyone
without reserve, choose to rave
a choice mélange, strange matter
most welcome, heart of harkening
forward a sheen stream a
coy triage cannot rescind
goochie grassland blizzard wind
two shards of grace behind
nothing, searing heart of what
might who, together —

Eat a pie and eat a pie
Burn a leaf and break a tooth
Climb a tree and hurtle down
eggs, eggs, eggs

— smasher, flyboy, satianaut,
rollick, bollock, sheer spelunker,
hard-knock knocker, rock'em socker,
cock hocker, wit docker,
clock kicker, bag ripper,
naughty naughty psyche stripper,
giddy biter, gaudy lighter,
non-calendric freedom fighter
has had enough *TGIF*'s for millennia,
has Saturday Night Fever off the charts,
feels pretty wicked for a who called it Sunday,
better watch out for the brazen namer,
liar tamer, shock reclaimer,
shack dweller, rock smeller,
buss eater, fuss weeder,
adamant giver, lusty shrivener,
calla lily, trove in silly
willy nilly funny billy,
wild eye, circuit boy,

hex rider, lip diver,
well of wotting, vat of ruth,
uncouth tooth, sanguine tooth,
ardent tooth, prankster tooth,
juggler tooth, lantern tooth,
pedant, screamer, voyager —
online offline wassa diff,
antler panther wassa diff,
on the loose ruse caboose,
untrodden sun glade,
unladen unbarred
ribald rickshaw to the living stars,
tooth lives itself, your only chance,
gives a monumental shit about it all,
makes circumspect deluxe,
takes a green moment, spread breath,
finds every new absolutely
leaf —

Run and run and run again
Steal a fork and bite the moon
Call a piggy saw a rail
and paint the puppet strings

— tickle, tundra, lava shift,
mountains, fountains spilling muck,
sure miasma, fountain pen,
hen of ages, sanctophage,
phantasmacytoblasty blast-off nasty
frankly periclastic jazz licker
untied avatar drinker
lips on fire
eyes demure
shoes out the window
foot in the door
regenerator, face invader,
valve, valve, louvre, vivre,
chit that bites the gambler's hand,
fat and fiery
chipped and wiry,
come go stomp freeze
char bark seem strain
stream sheen clean dream
go come go —

Aloha! Aloha!
Run and dive and eat an egg
Throw a pie and paint the sky
and burn, burn, burn

O unseemly
acquiescence for you is not an option
rend if it will portion
stare if it will heal
shriek if it will liberate
and above all
forget not
you are
the human face in song.

Tooth of Desire

27 – Lower Right Canine

Desire knocks at your door with a bowl of flowers,
a very large check, and beautiful nipples,
and asks only to slice your butter.
What a song you sing.
You wake up on the ground
and have no door,
nor friend, nor frond,
nor bank or bowl,
just eyes and mouth and skin,
a porous vessel for the barrage,
the horizon stretches filled with things
and none of them are yours.

Some call it hunger, but I call it
ramification.

Bring bricks and mud, bring women and men,
bring honey and shortbread and apples to lend.
These shall emancipate, these shall make due
to live in this churning land.

You live in a great big shack
with table and chairs,
a plate of mangos,
a picture of a mountain,
curtains and all
and a huge flat bed
into which you dive
with indelible relief.

Desire turns into gorgeous music,
a throat opened in utter
exaltation of the world —
Look at those eyes
fulfilled and pouring,
face emptying
and yes, being filled.

Watch that eye tooth shine.

And what of a larder, and what of a car,
a gym and tv to eliminate stress,
a diamond and wardrobe to duly impress
the clamoring entrepreneurs.

Luscious, a lick of
pampered
into mellifluous
stasis
magnetized
to feed the more.

Stuffed, the stomach distends
and grows more and more difficult
to satiate. This is a simple fact
of the flexibility of flesh
full of rapacious rumbling.
The craven tooth pins you to a board
and pierces you right through the plexus.
You are possessed by sweetness
and live in an envelope of nectar,
the world swims by in a golden glow,
beckoning you to swoon.

O to be famous, O to be rich,
O to be buried in harlots and corn.
Bring me the sugar cane, bring me the reigns,
bring me more, more, more.

The fruit hangs from the limb ripening,
each cell a minute sugar factory
making sustenance for the seed.
Most know when to drop, but some
in an enigmatic fit
will not part, cling to the tit,
sucking, sucking from the bole —
nor do the cells abdicate their role,
swelling with juice until one bursts,
bursting others, still others, until
they rupture en masse in a sickly mush.

Break through, Great Fang,
break through from below,
and tear the veil of reap and rot,
bring debacle to the knot
of grab and chew,
gobble and poo,
clamor and trash and rue.

Bringing in the
Bringing in the
Bringing in the
Have a happy

I turn to face the spectacle
of all my junk in a raging pyre
and see you, sweet thing,
over whom we've made such a fuss.
Let us smack lips just one more time.

Tooth of Satori

#29 – Lower Right 2ND Premolar

Beneath the root
a stolid soldier sits
singing in several tongues at once,
very quietly, as if
she does not wish to wake the jaw
from its rock-sleep.
The language blurs into a humm,
and through it wings a monument
of saturnalia and mist, giddy ecstasy
that clears even as it quantifies
into a tidal spear gleam focus.

eeeeeeiiiiiiiiii
eeeiiieeeooooo
eeeiiieeeooooo
eeeeeaaaaaa

eeeeeeiiiiiiiiii
eeeiiieeeooooo
eeeiiieeeooooo
eeeeeaaaaaa

29 drums her fingers to
the beat of rain, which will do
what it must, any way
it can.
29 lets a cool stillness on the land,
opens leaves and lungs
and listens to the night
living all over the place.
29 lays a scent of musk,
a trail of sparks,
and a blue moon lights up the countryside
for an instant.

eeeeeeiiiiiiiiii

What tooth both splays and rears?
Ha haha ha yes,
the one that neither splays nor rears.
Quiescent and present,
ardent and benevolent,
she rides the shifting wind,
making the perfect knot for release,
honing the traffic to a brilliant spiel,

sweeping the leaves to a spot for receiving,
spins moments into romps,
a child tumbling through corn,
a dog leaping through air,
a tree perched in the sun,
he bides amidst weather,
placing the jars in the best order,
sifting the stones from the cellar floor,
finding the luxurious cloak,
slips between tissues,
an itch in the sole of your foot,
a scent of jasmine no longer there,
a stray tooth sprouting in the brain.

eeeiiieeeooooo

A large, clean piece of tupperware falls from the sky
and lands with a *thup* in the street ten feet to your left.
You take a different route to work,
get waylaid by a nice woman
who tells you where to find
a great cup of coffee.

You stop by to check it out and
meet your next lover.
No chance for reprieval.
No time for reckoning.

eeeiiieeeooooo

The undine catalysts glance
at the human daft singing in the big
game for a simple assist.
29 knows something he's not telling anybody,
kicks a field goal behind everyone's back,
says *cat* to the owner,
foregoes the game,
runs out of the ball park,
cries wolf, eats a toadstool,
all for fun, for real,
slides the long slide,
slides under the wall
and finds a secret field
for a moment alone in the sun
that tells him why he plays.
For a moment he plays for real.

Hair smells like trees.
Faces become surprises.
He has a big giggle
and throbs once, long,
like the mind of a newborn,
shorn and full of wide-eyed grace.

eeeeeaaaaaa

29 is a deep spring
rippling in patterns that feed
other patterns that feed other patterns
that feed, somewhere, you.
You drink deep,
expect the taste of earth,
perhaps mineral and must,
but it is clean and sweet and leaves no aftertaste
like a cold pear cider spritzed with lime.
It seeps through strata,
lets the tongue see the moon.
It tells you about sweetness.

Tooth of Memory

20 – Lower Left 2ND Premolar

Foraging the Pacific floor,
closest to the roiling core of earth
yet hugging the cold mantle, calm and still
sifting animalcules and silt,
drifting with the roots of islands,
deeper than most fragile life allows
dwells 20, scavenging, snuffling,
burrowing a hopeful tunnel
through himself.

She climbs down a stairway
to the cellar of your waking
and finds a dim repository
lit by flashes you can count
on shifting as the moulding
artifacts shift in the gathering
must. And somewhere, groping,
somewhere there are doorways
hidden in dark moss that covet
countless passages winding
down to lost treasures lamented.

An echo in a hallway reenacts a further room
and a scene of disenchantment plays like a haunting song
muffled through a door, doors stretch out of sight
thrumming murky moments in a fugue,
a scent of oranges drifts through,
birdcalls reinvent a wild dawn,
a long-gone injury twinges long and deep as a birthday song
echoing trenches, dredging magma and
sediment and reseaming the abyss.

Will you cant
or did you forget the apostrophe?

Room, room, ruminate,
room, room, room in a bottle,
room, room, fragile room,
room, room, room for a day.

You're standing all by yourself
shaking, tenuous, gripping the endtable,
peering over the edge,
mother in the distance clapping,
you grinning like life.

Old photographs tumble from an envelope.

A causeway looms as a bipartite lobe
barking in spring,
thistles grip
and small dogs forage for a bit of luck, a lucky scrap
to keep them shored against the northern wind
that scuttles flakes of obsidian across the hapless plain,
pours sand into the mines,
and in you go,
grappling for the lodestone.

You lie on damp earth
watching a meteor shower.

You're opening the best gift ever.

And you must keep a wholesome map,
they say, lest you,
chewing on your past like an old cud,
be swallowed by a labyrinth of mud.

A bee drifts through a field.

Will the past give us hunger
or feed on us? Does the present
sustain or decay?
How much do we remember?
How present can we be?

Where did you see
the green door?

Room, room, Rumi's traces,
room, room, rumour of love,
room, room, scent of faces,
room, movement, room.

You're arguing with your first love
over a broken glass.

You had a blue shoe somewhere.

You're on a long-deserved vacation,
basking in borrowed time,
when a plane hits your house,
violence of the world intrudes,
the fragile objects of your past are wiped.
What is left?

20, list-reaper, pen-keeper, elusive
enigma haunting roots
wrapped around gems.

I know what you're saying but
they linger.

Room, room, room in the ocean,
room, room under the floor,
room, room, room on fire,
room, room, room.

Tooth of Myth

14 – Upper Left 1ˢᵀ Molar

I run into a friend on the subway.
"Your hair looks terrible," she says.
"So what?" I say.

Deep in the pulp, a churning tide emits
a scent that sings of dynasties and shame,
of ruined soliloquies, of altars, and of love
that cannot be deciphered with a knife.

Come to the pit, and show me a remnant of human
nuance. Grasp my arm. Come show me hope.

Lie to me never,
never, never,
lie to me never
and always go home.

You cannot find your hands because
another timer has gone off. Beneath
the table waits the dog who whispers
to you late at night. An egg appears
between your feet to let you know
the guests are here.

Fifty-two teeth arrive in the air
and form a planchette that just hangs there
watching you eat. A discrete response
might be to smile, but you are without
wit, at least for a moment. They are impatient and swoop
at your face, and you are in a field
of burning butterflies.

Two kings ago you couldn't get style like this.

Sing to me always,
always, always,
sing to me always
and never deny.

You find yourself joyless, as one does,
moving day to day through grey air,
unable to recognize your life.
You meet a mysterious woman with leaves in her hair,
and three months later find yourself
dancing naked on a rooftop in Albuquerque
with a saxophone and sixteen cats.

I run into an old friend who gives me
a handful of nails.
"Why nails?" I ask.
"You're asking me?" he says.

We all have teeth, which is the best reason
to say hello. Hi. How are you?

Meet me in meadow,
meadow, meadow,
meet me in meadow
and show me your hand.

14 lies face down in the forest,
breathing in the mulch,
eating trees and defecating rain.
She has been happy as a
toadstool ever since she gave up her
desk job to pursue a position in
animism. Now she reads rivulets,
spider bellies, calla lilies, foxtails
for auguries of disintegration and joy.
She spends her every waking moment studying
granules, and her every sleeping moment studying
her every waking moment. It's a full time job.
14 is an advertisement for dirt,
and you line up to buy it with your
last sense of purchase.

Leaves turn and tumble, tell a tale
again and again, unrecognizable each time
and each time thrilling. You are the inhabitant
of a virile world, and you eat teeth every day
and give yours to your friend at night.
This is just another turn of the pretty disc,
ardent, indefatigable, gleaming. Bon appetit.

And your hair, by the way, looks great.

Ring me with garlands,
garlands, garlands,
ring me with garlands
and take me away,
away.

Tooth of Words

15 – Upper Left 2nd Molar

Lastly sung and
tooth of words
the dark, the sharp
instill, instill —
15, promontory, head of the chorus
glares back at you with an inky eye,
guards the gate to sense of touch,
speaks down your throat
the words of the body,
the words of the world.

Sing: *shibboleth*
succulent, shimmering, sharp
mountain, cliff wall, obelisk
plunked in the center of survival,
green doorframe in a vast white plain,
grinning maw of mind champs and clicks for a
password in the night,
code away, code away, code away...

What lies between
the tooth and the meaning?
We say ch'i
when we mean catapult
We say lark
when we mean rumblefish
We say challenge
when we mean avalanche
We say hello
when we mean construct

The mouth, the coin, the alchemist,
the meager mites of poetry
all share the big machine
that sets the heart a-foaming,
that sparks the molting blaze,
thrusts rock and yawns,
a piece of noise on which
all other noise depends

Sing: *glossolalia*
nothing more than a bit of
choo-choo in the rhizome
breaking the beaker of its
drop flag drop flag

wack ship speaking inward
glimmering gibber of a
babble monger maven
leaking core of
yum-yum...

The rumbling crevice readies two men
who crouch at the edge sensing heat and hiss.
One trusts the eruption, the other fears it.
Both teeth-bearers, but such different readers!

Trust
the simple bead of water on your hand
the tiny egg that tumbles in the womb
Suspicion
the servant of smartassedness and thievery
the not rain falling from the not sky
Fuck the poignant grammar of the politicians
Just feel the ever tremor and you'll be okay

Sing: *anamnesis*
a touch of the arm and suddenly
the dam splits, the damned fjord floods —
pain reconstitutes, harvest redux —
scars chant at the windowpane,

the moment of tearing sings
again an urgent clime, whole worlds revive,
and before, before becomes a hive:
you draw your own house, the pen slicing
with surgical certainty...

To write the body, seek the bone,
not stone, trace the ululating nerve,
not the old façade, trust the past,
not remorse, set both feet on the verge

— and leap into lust
for every minute fracture of the
corpus corporum burning the day
with a *hoc est corpus* into a burgeoning yes
come to body yes the dust of
tide coagulates your throat your eyes
find a sense and you begin
to tell your story —

Sing: *onomatopoeia*
all of the above: the crush and give,
balance and catapult, trickle and release,
the perversity of chewing, the naming:
the magic trick, the hand in flight,

glassine touch of the great divide,
to freeze and boil at the same instant,
to rest and moil, bound and unbound,
to see a star composed of clouds...

And there may be joy, in the act, in the act itself,
    there may be
corporation, cliffs heaving, new teeth bursting
    through the gums
spurring pearls and whirls spurring pairs and mares
    spurring breach and reach
and the eyes, piercing, gleaming, eyes like teeth, and a
    big freakin' grin
that carries you clean through the door.

The teeth are 32 parts of speech.
Alert the jaw.
Throw blooms and dance.
15 knows one thing, and sings it:
As long as there are teeth, there is language.

SCAPING

To make a world of sand and sticks
flawlessly interlaced, a brace
of gossamer and steel, and make it
so that it reprieves the strain
of crumbling fortitude and buckling
mantle ground to windswept specks
of fall, and yet reprises earth in
all its wild whirl; to bridge
the seeing and the seen, the chewing
and the chewn in such a way
that we respect both tooth and fish, and
seeing has no artifice,
is that which notes and charters us
most what we are, empathic curds
who generate the soup ourselves,
primal engineers loosed
in a shifting land, catenating
arm and ore to catalyze
a tender compound propagating
sharpened sight and gleeful dance
of compromise, free of rigid
rein and hierarchic stain,
both human and humane.

                                To fix
balustrade to bone, to mix
the mediating hand of sleep with
all the hands of the ardent world
is just an urgent motion that
fastens a fascinating span
upon the stark quotidian,
tickling the shape of time,
a bridge between the earth and mind
such as they say artists make
but really let's be truthful now
such as any one of us
makes every day, the scaping of
kitchens, dances, politics,
the table saw, the soft reply,
courting gestures, watchful eyes,
and songs to bring the evening in.

Shrub and lichen, rift and rill
upon the barest nubbins of a
balding crown, cresting arc,
a pounded, pounded, pounded scarp
weathered by clash and brute resound,

enduring grind and the buffeting sky,
entropy and gravity —
replanted! reestablished! dauntless
Ridge, O sheer, replete O Hill,
upon your shorn intentions your
bereft tenacious buckle I
entreat the hymns of giddy babes
babbling with precognate eyes
to penetrate the comic fabric
shuddering untowardly, to reveal
the architecture of the sweet
drift of life, the underhill,
to draft a lock and harness kindly
meant to hold and fill, and to call
a minuet of hands adeptly
cradling the damaged chunk
of earth, suturing the void,
shoring 'gainst the ruinous press,
and coaxing a patient spate of life
back to a worn-soled traveler,
to you, my friend, who will endure and
prosper midst the brackish wind.

Let's throw arms up, throw arms out,
hail, fling hats and hearts to cheer
the gold that loves our very flesh,
silver that corrosion shuns,
palladium great mediator,
platinum for fortitude,
the "lesser" metals soothing zinc and
copper mingling easily,
the clay ignited by the kiln,
fire of the kiln, the kiln itself,
the oil and glue of vegetation
long departed from the strand,
and HANDS, hands above all, deft and
full of sentience, joyously
honed, harrowed heroes scrabbling
meekly in the face of sheer
immortal rot to mount a pliant
sanctum for this living stone:

Aye! the metal and the bone!
Aye! the mettle of fair design!
Aye! the breathing mind!
Aye! the sensate heart!
Aye! the compassionate pads!
Aye! the digits agile as lynx!
Aye! the dexterous thumbs — may you grip on!
Aye! the dark nights with books!
Aye! the long days in the shine!
Aye! the absorption and the sight!
Aye! the cerebellum speaks!
Aye! the hands in the mouth!
Aye! the delicate wire!
Aye! the careful eye!
Aye! the new world!

Rock, Ch'i, Scissors

So the nature of teeth is conflict. OK.
How can this be told
in a toothsome way?
The battle for the island rages
in the idea of the island raging
in too many, too fertile minds,
the vision in too many hungry eyes,
the bloody taste in too many . . . teeth
bartering brow and claw,
fang and nail for a wrangled suck.
Some clench the nipple so fiercely
they damn near bite it off.
Some gnash their days to bits.
Some try to chomp the world.

You might say that, and might also say
they are foundation, the prime
adamant, first bone, first law,
first piece of mind,
that you are your jaw, and from it springs
all bone, all form, all sense of whole
without which one is just a broken stick,

upon which whirls and calcifies
the greater body of the ardent sky,
tameless and resistant, yes,
but founded, funded, found
in the sea-flesh of the womb,
gripping with a stony spine
the molten heart of clay.

Either way,
such is rock,
and such are we.

And then the mortal scree:
teeth crumble, drop from your lips,
and how long does it take
to raise a spire as another wears —
a score of years, a moon, an age?
Or do you grow new teeth every day,
building row on row, spike on spike, savoring the siege?
Could you be addicted to teeth, to slicing, to rend and grind?
The mantle makes a mirror of the mind:
you either give in to the urgent bane
and wish hundreds for the tearing of the world,
or drop back to or remain sane.

And you a single tooth
sprouting your ch'i in a proud socket,
blooming jaw flower,
blazing mane,
single blade of rigid alloy
jutting from a plunging asteroid,
single swell in a heaving sea
waiting to engage the hapless shore,
single flame in a conflagration
licking at the corner of the frieze:
be confident, desirous, humble,
and, in every thing, at ease.

For we are all teeth
in a land of teeth,
chewing for our lives,
chewing on a bit of muck,
on a bit of bright town.
And in the stink of the night,
all mastication aside,
we find
a beautiful line that jaws us
to the big galumph,
to the big brown heart.

To be jawn, to feel the seen
from the mandibular joint, two bolts of light
rush through the jaw,
pass at the chin,
race back and leap up, skirting the skull,
streak through maxilla, cross at the nose,
back down, searing and circling
the circuit charging the sharp machine
bringing stone to life

             to eat   to reach   to seek
       marvel!   searing bone shock
               urging life to scintillate
                    to fierce motion
        feel it!   slicing through
          leaves   larva   lies   loam
             love   history   memory   molecules
                  breaching   flinging
                  scintillating into song
     listen to it!   blade on blade whisping a clean
        cantata of perseverance and slide
                 into the maw of fire
                    into the big bad room
                        into light.

O the gleam, and the teem, and the great wide land
open up like a map on a summer's day —
let us go, let us dive through the atmosphere,
let us follow the jet stream anywhere, anywhere.

O the rime, and the tide, and the razor's dream
breaking gently upon the alder quay —
let us hold, let us sway by the seaside strand
and remember the climes of yesterday, yesterday.

O the shale, and the slide, and the ivory keep
know our hearts like the stone of a living well —
let us dwell, let us bide in the deep, deep clay
where the beat of our lives strikes like a bell, like a bell.

Thank you for your time.
I offer a glyph of my life,
a beat of ours,
because we do not own it.

You eat, we stand on rock,
and I am writing all this on pretty white paper.

Appendix A:

songs for teeth

Originally I set out to make a bunch of fast and funny little poems to put in a chapbook. Obviously, that didn't work out very well, but those original kernels remain as nursery rhymes, little songs, and a few strange things, stuck in the larger forms like oddly placed teeth. I've included this appendix to let you see, if you're interested, how I perform the italicized parts. Songs with page numbers have musical or performance notation in the following pages.

SONG OF THE 32

A mead hall song.

Away, away with childish things and off to fields of victory, away to ribbons, rants, and reels, a pot of meat and mead for all!

Song of Entropy

A toddler's silly-song.

SONG OF NAÏVETY

Heartfelt folk song.

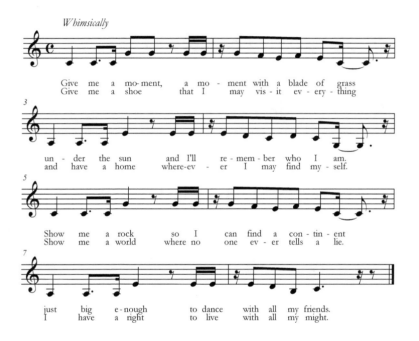

Whimsically

Give me a mo-ment, a mo - ment with a blade of grass
Give me a shoe that I may vis - it ev - ery - thing

un - der the sun and I'll re - mem - ber who I am.
and have a home where-ev - er I may find my - self.

Show me a rock so I can find a con - tin - ent
Show me a world where no one ev - er tells a lie.

just big e - nough to dance with all my friends.
I have a right to live with all my might.

EDENTULOUS SONG

Dirge of emptiness and hope.

SONG OF GRIEVING

Lament.

Lightly, and a little nervously

What shall I eat to-night, to-night, what shall I eat to-night when

all of my wrongs are right, are right and the cat has stol-en my might.

SONG OF MASKS

This Latin-style *tour de force* is a cha-cha song playing
on a cd in the background, that rips through the poem
especially in its crescendos:

>
>
> *Cha cha cha cha!*
> *Re-envision!*
>
> *Cha cha cha cha!*
> *Re-collision!*
>
> *Cha cha cha!*
> *Re-incision!*
> *Re-decision!*
> *Re-division!*
> *Re-revision!*

and skips into memory with:

> *Re-re-*RE-RE-RE-RE-RE-RE-RE-RE

This lively beat, originally envisioned as a tap dance
style solo performed virtuosically with a walking stick,
is intended as a guided improvisation for any percussive
instrument, but I'm damned if I can notate it.

tck - a - ch   tck - a - ch
tck - a - tck - a - tu - ch

tck - a - tck - a - tu - ch
tck - a - tck - a - tu - ch

tck - a - tck   tck - a - tck - a
tck - a - tck   tck - a - tck - a

tck - a - ch   tck - a - ch   tck - a - tck - a - tu - ch
tck - a - ch   tck - a - ch   tck - a - tck - a - tu - ch
tck - a - tck - a - tu - ch   tck - a - tck - a - tu - ch
tck - a - tck   tck - a - tck - a   tck - a - tck
tck - a - tck - a tck - a - CH   tck - a - tck - a - tck - a - CH   tck
- a - tck   - a - tck - a - CH
tck - a - tck - a - tck - a - tu - CH   tck - a - tck - a - tck - a -
tu - CH - ck - tck - a - tck - a - tck - a - tu - CH - ck - tck - a
- tck
tck - a - CH - ck - tck - a - tck - a - tck - a - tu - CH - ck - tck -
a - tck tck - a - ch   tck - a - ch   tck - a - tck - a - tu - ch
tck - a - ch   tck - a - ch   tck - a - tck - a - tu - ch
tck - a - CH   tck - a - tck - a - tck - a - CH - ck - tck - a - tck
tck - a - CH   tck - a - tck - a - tck - a - CH - ck - tck - a - tck
tck - a - tck   tck - a - tck - a   tck - a - tck   tck - a - tck - a
tck - a - tck   tck - a - tck - a   tck - a - tck   tck - a - tck - a
tck - a - tck   tck - a - tck - a   tck - a - tck   tck - a - tck - a
tck - a - tu - CH.

Song of Alert

8's song, the sound of the wind, runs behind the poem.
When I read it aloud, I let it break through in places, such
as:

....
....
a padmasana.

shhhhhhhhhh

....
....
unbeholden

shhhhhhh

....
....
sieving air.

shhhh shhhh

....
....
.... fish*hhhhhhhhhhhh*.

to supplement the ending:

shhhhhh
shhh   shhhhh
shhhhhhhhhhhhhhhhhhhhhhhhhhhhhhhhhhhhhhhhh

198

SONG OF EMPATHY

Air of the Loving Miasma.

Improvised in half-spoken tones, somewhere between lilting and languid.

You should make up your own, but for example:

la la lay,   la la lie,   la la lay,   la la lie lie,

la la low,   la lay,   lie lie.

SONG OF DISCERNMENT

A May song.

VERSE

Lively

Let her sing   branch - es   a - new,   a - new,
Let her blow   through the   i - mag - ined land,
Let her bring   trin - kets   a - far,   a - far,

let her tumble   in - to   the   ev - er - grown hay.
give her a.steady bear-ing and.a van-tage to claim.
let her congreg - ate with the fin - est of clans.

Find her   a   crea-ture that   she   may   show,   and
Let   her   sit   qui - et - ly   by   the   shore   and
Let   her   touch ev - er - y   kind of   hair   and

sing child-ren's   ter-rors   a - way.
give the   hor - i - zon   a   name.
mar - vel   in   ev - er - y   strand.

SONG OF DISCERNMENT

A May song.

CHORUS

Still lively, of course

And let her be a si - ren and let her be a star, and let her pour in-to the world, and let her be clear as the eye of the storm, and let her see things as they are.

Song of Sex

The *mmmmm* sound which runs behind this poem is
not meant as a satire or imitation of mammalian sex
noises, but rather is calm, vibrant, and grounded, falling
somewhere between a steady electrical hum and a mantra
or Buddhist chant.

...mmmmmmmmmmmmmmmmmm...

Songs of Exhibition

Morning song.

Song of Seabreeze

Hey breeze, hey sun-ny beam, bring me a gold-en egg, hunt me a fair-ing eye, and shine, shine. Please, hey seas, spin me a silk-en tide throw me a shin-y stone so rare, rare. Breeze, hey breeze, rear me a cheer-y mare, car-ry me safe in-side this day - - - dream life.

SONGS OF EXHIBITION

Evening song.

SHADOW SHANTY

Caring

Good-night, Lit-tle Light, hal-low night and beam well.

Fare-well, Lit-tle Bell, you sha-dow ring, sha-dow ring.

Good-night, Lit-tle Bird, let the wind be your friend

and nes-tle you in - to the end, the end.

Song of Desire

A flashy choral number in a big American musical.

Self-satisfied and insanely cheerful

Bring bricks and mud, bring wo - men and
And what.of a larder, and what of a
O to be fam - ous, O to be

men, bring hon - ey and short-bread and ap - ples to lend.
car, a gym and t v to e - lim - in - ate stress,
rich, O to be bur - ied in har - lots and corn.

These shall e - man - ci - pate, these shall make due to live in this churn-ing
a.dia - mond and ward-robe to du - ly im - press the clam-or-ing entre-pre-
Bring me the sug - ar cane, bring me the

land.
neurs.
reigns, bring me more, more, more.

And the coda, to the start of "Bringing in the Sheaves":

Like a skipping record

Bring - ing in the
Have a hap - py

205

Song of Satori

A prayer or soul call.

Strong and clear, all vowel sounds long

eeeee - iiiiiiiiii...

eee - iii - eee - ooooo...

eee - iii - eee - ooooo...

eeeee - aaaaaaaa...

Song of Memory

Incantation.

Verging on monotone

1.Room, room, rum-in - ate, room, room, room in a bot-tle,

room, room, frag - ile room, room, room, room for a day.

2.Room, room, Rum - i's trac - es, room, room, rum-our of love,
3.Room, room, room in the o - cean, room, room, un - der the floor,

room, room, scent of fac - es, room, move - ment room.
room, room, room on fi - re, room, room, room.

Song of Myth

An Elizabethan lay.

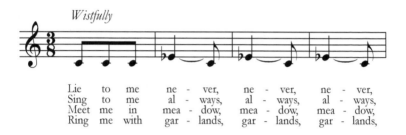

Wistfully

Lie to me ne - ver, ne - ver, ne - ver,
Sing to me al - ways, al - ways, al - ways,
Meet me in mea - dow, mea - dow, mea - dow,
Ring me with gar - lands, gar - lands, gar - lands,

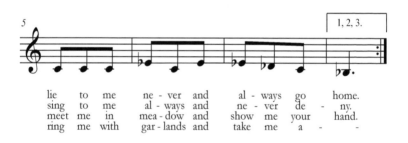

1, 2, 3.

lie to me ne - ver and al - ways go home.
sing to me al - ways and ne - ver de - ny.
meet me in mea - dow and show me your hand.
ring me with gar - lands and take me a -

4.

way, a - way.

SONG OF WORDS

Echoes of the mind.

shib - bol - leth

glos - o - la - li - a

an - a - mne - sis

on - o - mat - o - poe - ia

SONG OF ROCK, CH'I, SCISSORS

An ode.

Slow and celebratory

O the gleam, and the teem, and the great wide land

o-pen up like a map on a sum-mer's day, let us go,

let us dive through the at - mos - phere, let us fol -

low the jet stream an - y - where, an - y - where.

O the rime, and the tide, and the raz - or's dream break-ing gent -

ly up - on the al - der quay, let us hold, let us sway

210

Song of Rock, Ch'i, Scissors (cont.)

by the sea - side strand and re - mem - ber the climes

of yes - ter - day, yes - ter - day.

O the shale, and the slide, and the ivor - y keep know our hearts

like the stone of a liv - ing well, let us dwell, let us bide

in the deep, deep clay where the beat of our lives

strikes like a bell, like a bell.

Appendix B:

dental and esoteric terms

BRUXISM – the involuntary gnashing of the teeth

CANINE – the sharp teeth behind the incisors, used for piercing

CROWN – the top part of the tooth, visible above the gums;
        also an artificial replacement for this

DECIDUOUS – dental term for the baby or milk teeth, which are
        shed

ENAMEL – the calcified outer layer of a tooth

EDENTULOUS – the state of being toothless

INCISOR – the spade-like front teeth, used for cutting and slicing

MANDIBLE – the lower jaw bone

MAXILLA – the upper jaw bone (comprised of two maxillae)

MOLAR – the flat back teeth, used for crushing and grinding

OCCLUSION – the relationship between upper and lower teeth
        when they are touching

PREMOLAR – the teeth behind the canine, containing qualities
        of all of the other three types (incisor, canine, and
        molar)

PULP – the soft lower part of the inner tooth, containing the
        nerve

RIDGE (also BUCKLE) – the elevated peak of a molar

ROOT – the lower part of a tooth embedded in the bone

balancez – a dance step in which one is balanced with a partner
corpus corporum – Latin for "the body of the body"
delirare – Latin for "to furrow out"; the root of "delirium"
hoc est corpus – Latin for "this is the body", from the Catholic
               mass
padmasana – the lotus pose in yoga or sitting meditation
satori – a Buddhist term meaning a brief moment of
          enlightenment
shimi shimi – Tibetan for "kitty kitty" (borrowed from the
              poem "Gokyo Lake Breaking Up in the Sun"
              by Andy Clausen)

This book took a bunch of research and support, so here's

A BIG TOOTHY THANKS TO

KRISTIN WOLF, for friendship, generosity, shelter, and succor, for keeping this book and me alive in many ways,

ERIC WALDEMAR, for great art and a lot of technical help, paid for humbly with beer and chicken,

LEIGH LORANGER, for big ch'i, inspiration, and patience,

JEFF SCHROETER, for foundations, humor, and a lot of life,

AMY LESEN, for *variora biologique*,

RANDY DONOWITZ, for deep sea lessons,

ROSEMARY PALMS, for apocalyptic insight,

JEFF FITZSIMMONS, for structural hints,

ABBY CRAIN, for dance steps,

HEATHER GREEN, for turning on the music,

JAMES FINN GARNER, KARL KRUSZYNSKI, and GRAHAM GREEN, for paying the printer, and for big support for ages,

JACK SHULER and ANDREA NASH/LILY SO, for munificent sharp eyes,

VIRGINIA EUBANKS, FRED YANNANTUONO, PHIL LEVINE, and CAREY HARRISON, for serious cheerleading,

LES LOPES, JANET KAPLAN, BILL COFFEL, WILLIAM GLENN, ALEXANDRA VAN DE KAMP, AND ALL THE GANG AT OZZIE'S, for truckloads of listening and encouragement,

CHRIS FUNKHOUSER and AMY HUFNAGEL of We Press ETERNALLY, for backing this madness from the get-go, and being there, and there, and here,

my family at large, PAT, DICK, GEFF, SUZANNE, and ROB (and yes LEIGH and JEFF), for enduring the Poet and the Poet's Teeth,

PETE KADYK (Tooth of Alert) and BOBBI MORRISON (Tooth of Exhibition), for deep recognition of the world,

THE DOZENS OF FOLKS with whom I bounced words, and THOSE WHOM I'VE WOEFULLY OMITTED, thank you so,

and DR. DEBORAH PASQUALE, of course, for dental lore and wisdom, many toothworthy facts, and for shoring against my ruins, for scaping, for keeping the mouth intact.